SUDAN 2016 HUMAN RIGHTS REPORT

EXECUTIVE SUMMARY

Sudan is a republic with power concentrated in the hands of authoritarian President Omar Hassan al-Bashir and his inner circle. The National Congress Party (NCP) maintained control of the government, continuing 27 years of near-absolute political authority. The country last held national elections (presidential and National Assembly) in April 2015. Key opposition parties boycotted the elections when the government failed to meet their preconditions, including a cessation of hostilities, holding of an inclusive "national dialogue," and fostering of an environment conducive to discussions between the government and opposition on needed reforms and the peace process. In the period prior to the elections, security forces arrested many supporters, members, and leaders of boycotting parties and confiscated numerous newspapers, conditions that observers said created a repressive environment not conducive to free and fair elections. Only 46 percent of eligible voters participated in the elections, according to the government-controlled National Electoral Commission (NEC), but others believed the turn out to have been much lower. The NEC declared President Bashir winner of the elections with 94 percent of the votes.

Civilian authorities at times did not maintain effective control over the security forces. Some armed elements did not openly identify with a particular security entity, making it difficult to determine under whose control they operated. In January 2015 the NCP absolute-majority parliament broadened the mandate of the National Intelligence and Security Services (NISS) to include authorities previously reserved for the armed forces.

Since January 2014 the president has led a national dialogue process aimed at solving the country's internal political and social challenges. In October the political forces participating in the national dialogue concluded the process by signing the National Document, which includes the general features of a future constitution to be finalized by transitional institutions. Most opposition groups boycotted the process; many doubted the government's commitment to genuine dialogue and peacebuilding. Meanwhile, parallel negotiations between the government and other opposition movements continued primarily under auspices of the African Union High-level Implementation Panel (AUHIP).

In March the government unilaterally signed the AUHIP "Roadmap" in a move toward consensus on a monitored cessation of hostilities and humanitarian access.

On June 17, President Bashir declared a four-month unilateral cessation of hostilities in Blue Nile and South Kordofan (the "Two Areas") and an end to offensive military actions in Darfur. In August key armed movements and holdout opposition parties signed onto the AUHIP Roadmap. In October, President Bashir extended the ceasefire for a two-month period; on December 31, he declared a one-month extension of its cessation of hostilities in conflict zones.

The three most significant human rights problems were inability of citizens to choose their government, aerial bombardments of civilian areas by military forces and attacks on civilians by government and other armed groups in conflict zones, and abuses perpetrated by NISS with impunity through special security powers given it by the regime. On January 14, the government launched an intensive aerial and ground offensive against Sudan Liberation Army-Abdul Wahid (SLA/AW) strongholds in the Jebel Marra area of Darfur. This operation displaced more than 44,700 persons by January 31, according to the UN Office for the Coordination of Humanitarian Affairs (OCHA). In February the government established in Darfur a suboffice of the National Human Rights Commission to enhance the commission's capacity to monitor human rights in Darfur. Meanwhile, ground forces comprising Rapid Support Forces (RSF) and Border Guards carried out attacks against more than 50 villages in an attempt to dislodge the armed opposition. Attacks on villages often included killing and beating of civilians; sexual and gender-based violence; forced displacement; looting and burning entire villages; destroying food stores and other infrastructure necessary for sustaining life; and attacks on humanitarian targets, including humanitarian facilities and peacekeepers. In September, Amnesty International issued a report alleging that, through September the government engaged in scorched-earth tactics and used chemical weapons in Jebel Marra, Darfur. UN monitors were unable to verify the alleged use of chemical weapons, due in part to lack of access to Jebel Marra, including by rebel commanders loyal to Abdel Wahid. By year's end the Organization for the Prohibition of Chemical Weapons (OPCW) had not been presented with sufficient corroborating evidence to conclude chemical weapons had been used.

The NISS continued to show a pattern of widespread disregard for rule of law, committing major abuses, such as extrajudicial and other unlawful killings; torture, beatings, rape and other cruel or inhuman treatment or punishment; arbitrary arrest and detention by security forces; harsh and life-threatening prison conditions; incommunicado detention; prolonged pretrial detention; obstruction of humanitarian assistance; restrictions on freedom of speech, press, assembly, association, religion, and movement; and intimidation and closure of human rights and nongovernmental organizations (NGOs).

Societal abuses included discrimination against women; sexual violence; female genital mutilation/cutting (FGM/C); early childhood marriage; use of child soldiers; child abuse; sexual exploitation of children; trafficking in persons; discrimination against ethnic and religious minorities, persons with disabilities, and persons with HIV/AIDS; denial of workers' rights; and child labor.

Government authorities did not investigate human rights violations by NISS, the military or any other branch of the security services, with limited exceptions relating to the national police. The government failed to adequately compensate families of victims of shootings during the September 2013 protests, make its investigations public, or hold security officials accountable. Impunity remained a problem in all branches of the security forces.

Section 1. Respect for the Integrity of the Person, Including Freedom from:

a. Arbitrary Deprivation of Life and other Unlawful or Politically Motivated Killings

There were numerous reports government forces and ethnic militia groups committed arbitrary and unlawful killings of civilians in connection with the conflicts in Darfur and the Two Areas. Unlike previous years, abuses in Abyei were mostly the result of intercommunal violence.

Security forces used fatal excessive force against civilians, demonstrators, and detainees, including in the conflict zones (see section 1.g.).

On January 31, NISS agents detained Salah Gamar Ibrahim, a Darfuri student aligned with a Sudan Liberation Army-Abdel Wahid (SLA/AW)-affiliated student political organization, following a political forum. According to family members, NISS agents "dumped [him] in a critical state" outside his family's home that same day. His family immediately took him to the hospital, where the next day a doctor recommended transferring him from Darfur to Khartoum for further treatment. NISS rejected the request, and Ibrahim died the same day. As of year's end, the government had not released results of an investigation.

There were numerous abuses reported similar to the following examples: On April 20, the administration of Kordofan University ordered the closure of the university indefinitely due to the killing of student Abu Baker Hashim reportedly by the NISS during April 19 university student elections in El Obeid, North Kordofan. The school remained closed until July 31, when it reopened with a heavily armed police presence. On April 28, al-Ahlia Omdurman University ordered the school's indefinite closure due to the killing of student Mohammed al-Sadig in April 27 clashes between progovernment and opposition students on campus. No investigations were made public.

In 2014 security forces used force and live ammunition to disperse students at the University of Khartoum protesting escalating violence in Darfur. One student, Ali Abakar Musa Idris, died of injuries. As of year's end, the government had not released any report on the incident.

In August 2015 the government announced it would compensate families of the victims of the September 2013 protests. The Sudan Advisory Council for Human Rights reported that 81 of 85 families had agreed to accept financial compensation, while four requested authorities to open court cases. Observers estimated 200 deaths resulted from the protests. According to the government, families not initially identified for compensation were eligible for compensation if a court so decided. It was not clear this decision was publicly known. In November 2015 media reported that the Ministry of Justice had allocated three million Sudanese pounds (SDG) ($450,000) to compensate the families of the 85 identified victims killed in the protests, equivalent to 40,000 SDG ($6,000) for each victim. In addition 35 million SDG ($5.3 million) would go toward compensating victims who suffered property damage. Some members of parliament recommended postponing compensation until perpetrators of the crimes were brought to justice. Other members suggested that neither compensation nor criminal prosecutions were needed because the security forces were acting in official capacities. As of August the government had not released a report on the events of September 2013, and no lawyers representing the victims' families reported that any of the claimants had been compensated. A prominent activist published an article challenging the government to publish the name of one compensated family member. The government gave no response. A lawyer for one family reported that most families preferred justice and accountability for perpetrators rather than compensation.

During the year President Bashir continued to have two outstanding warrants for arrest against him based on International Criminal Court (ICC) indictments in 2009 and 2010 for genocide, war crimes, and crimes against humanity in Darfur. Nonetheless, Bashir still traveled by invitation to countries including Ethiopia,

China, Egypt, Saudi Arabia, Uganda, Chad, Rwanda, Mauritania, Djibouti, Morocco, Equatorial Guinea, and the United Arab Emirates.

b. Disappearance

There were reports of politically motivated disappearances. As in prior years, this included disappearances in non-conflict (as well as conflict) areas.

On May 5, nine University of Khartoum student protesters were seeking legal counsel at the office of lawyer Nabil Adeeb when NISS personnel forcibly entered, severely beat Adeeb's staff and clients, and took the students and one staff member to unknown locations, later revealed to be NISS facilities in Khartoum and Omdurman. NISS arrested six more student protesters from their and their friends' homes. Following domestic and international pressure, all 14 students were released. They all reported suffering physical and verbal abuse while in NISS custody, and some showed visible signs of torture. As of November, a 15th student, Asim Omer, who was arrested separately on the University of Khartoum campus, remained in custody and had been charged with murder of a police officer. Trials were underway, although delayed considerably.

According to the government, NISS maintained public information offices to receive inquiries about missing or detained family members. Families of missing or detained persons often reported that such inquiries went unanswered. In November and December, the government detained dozens of persons in front of witnesses but later refused to confirm that it had custody of any of them. In some instances, national police admitted arrest and transfer of persons to NISS custody, but NISS later would not admit custody.

There were no developments in the alleged NISS abduction of political activist Sandra Kadouda in April 2015.

Government forces and armed criminal elements were responsible for the disappearance of civilians, humanitarian workers, and UN and other international personnel in conflict areas (see section 1.g.).

c. Torture and Other Cruel, Inhuman, or Degrading Treatment or Punishment

The 2005 Interim National Constitution prohibits torture and cruel, inhuman, and degrading treatment, but security forces, government-aligned groups, rebel groups, and ethnic factions continued to torture, beat, and harass suspected political opponents, rebel supporters, and others.

In accordance with the government's interpretation of sharia (Islamic law), the penal code provides for physical punishments, including flogging, amputation, stoning, and the public display of a body after execution, despite the constitution's prohibitions. With the exception of flogging, such physical punishment was rare. Courts routinely imposed flogging, especially as punishment for the production or consumption of alcohol.

The law requires police and the attorney general to investigate deaths on police premises, regardless of suspected cause. Reports of suspicious deaths in police custody were sometimes investigated but not prosecuted. For example, in November authorities detained a man upon his return from Israel. He died while in custody, allegedly from falling out a window, although the building had sealed windows.

The president called on the chief prosecutor and chief justice to ensure full legal protection of police carrying out their duties and stated that police should investigate police officers only when they were observed exceeding their authority.

Government security forces (including police, NISS, and military intelligence personnel of the Sudanese Armed Forces (SAF)) beat and tortured physically and psychologically persons in detention, including members of the political opposition, civil society, religious activists, and journalists, according to civil society activists in Khartoum, former detainees, and NGOs. Torture and other forms of mistreatment included prolonged isolation, exposure to extreme temperature variations, electric shock, and use of stress positions. Some female detainees alleged NISS harassed and sexually assaulted them. Some former detainees reported being injected with an unknown substance without their consent. Many former detainees, including detained students, reported being forced to take sedatives that caused lethargy and severe weight loss. The government subsequently released many of these persons without charge.

Government authorities detained members of the Darfur Students Association during the year. Upon release, numerous students showed visible signs of severe physical abuse. Government forces reportedly used live bullets to disperse crowds of protesting Darfuri students. There were numerous reports of violence against student activists' family members.

Security forces detained political opponents incommunicado, without charge, and tortured them. Some political detainees were held in isolation cells in regular prisons, and many were held without access to family or medical treatment. Human rights organizations asserted NISS ran "ghost houses," where it detained opposition and human rights figures without acknowledging they were being held. Such detentions at times were prolonged.

Journalists were beaten, threatened, and intimidated (see section 2.a.).

The law prohibits (what it deems as) indecent dress and punishes it with a maximum of 40 lashes, a fine, or both. Officials acknowledged authorities applied these laws more frequently against women than men and applied them to both Muslims and non-Muslims. Courts denied some women bail, although by law they may have been eligible.

There were numerous abuses reported similar to the following example: On June 25, the Public Order Police arrested several young women and men in Khartoum under the Public Order Act for "indecent dress." During the sweep, all women who did not have their hair covered were taken into custody. The Public Order Police further arrested two young men for wearing shorts. According to NGO reports, the Public Order Police released the young women and men later the same day without charges.

Security forces, rebel groups, and armed individuals perpetrated sexual violence against women throughout the country; the abuse was especially prevalent in the conflict areas (see section 1.g.).

As of year's end, no investigations into the allegations of mass rape in Thabit, Darfur, had taken place (see section 6).

Prison and Detention Center Conditions

The Ministry of Interior generally does not release information on the physical conditions of prisons. Information about the number of juvenile and female prisoners was unavailable.

<u>Physical Conditions</u>: Prison conditions throughout the country remained harsh, overcrowded, and life threatening. The Prisons and Reform Directorate, a branch of the national police that reports to the Ministry of Interior, oversees prisons. According to human rights activists and released detainees, military intelligence

officials also detained civilians on military installations, especially in conflict areas.

Overall conditions, including food, sanitary and living conditions, were reportedly better in women's detention facilities and prisons, such as the Federal Prison for Women in Omdurman, than at equivalent facilities for men, such as Kober or Omdurman Prisons. In Khartoum juveniles were not held in adult prisons or jails, but they were reportedly held with adults elsewhere.

Prison health care, heating, ventilation, and lighting were often inadequate. Some prisoners did not have access to medications or physical examinations. Authorities generally provided food, water, and sanitation to prisoners, although the quality of all three was basic. Whereas prisoners previously relied on family or friends for food, families were no longer allowed to provide food or other items to family members. Most prisoners did not have beds. Ventilation and lighting conditions differed between prisons. Overcrowding was a major problem.

There were reports of deaths due to negligence in prisons and pretrial detention centers, but comprehensive figures were not available. Local press reported deaths resulting from suspected torture by police (see section 1.a.). Human rights advocates reported that additional deaths resulted from harsh conditions, such as extreme heat and lack of water, at military detention facilities.

In March the Sudan News Agency reported the Ministry of Justice would release 1,749 inmates to alleviate overcrowding. The releases included 431 inmates from Dabak Prison, 70 from Kober Prison, 84 from Omdurman Men's Prison, 521 women with 107 children from the Omdurman Women's Prison, 479 from Sob and Jeriaf Prisons, and 164 from al-Huda Prison. Whether those released included political prisoners or captured rebels was not known.

In March media reported that Nyala Prison, built to accommodate 650 inmates, held more than 1,000 inmates.

Authorities regularly denied prisoners held in NISS facilities visits from family and lawyers and, in the case of foreign prisoners, from foreign government representatives. Some former detainees reported security forces held them incommunicado; beat them; deprived them of food, water, and toilets; and forced them to sleep on cold floors.

Political prisoners were held in special sections of prisons. The main prison in Khartoum, Kober Prison, contained separate sections for political prisoners, those convicted of financial crimes, and others. NISS holding cells in Omdurman prisons were known to local activists as "the fridges" due to the extremely cold-controlled temperatures and the lack of windows and sunlight.

The number of deaths in prison was unknown. On August 18, the *Sudan Tribune* newspaper reported five Justice and Equality Movement/Debajo (JEM/D) faction rebel detainees died of tuberculosis due to neglect, overcrowding, and prison authorities' refusal to send prisoners for treatment.

Detainees reported physical violence by guards. Political detainees reported facing harsher treatment. One former detainee recounted being forced to beat a fellow-detainee while both were blindfolded. He stated he did not know who he was beating until the other detainee screamed in pain. Other former detainees recounted hours-long beating sessions during which NISS agents reportedly rounded up multiple prisoners, moved them to a large room, beat them with closed fists, and struck them with weapons.

Rebel groups in Darfur and the Two Areas reportedly detained persons in isolated locations in prison-like detention centers.

Administration: It was difficult to confirm prison administrative records were complete and accurate, as the government considered such information confidential and did not release it. Prison officials reportedly did not always know how many inmates NISS held in prisons.

Police reportedly allowed some visitors, including lawyers and family members, while prisoners were in custody and during judicial hearings. Political detainees and other prisoners held in NISS custody seldom were allowed visits from lawyers or family members, despite repeated requests for access. Visitors generally were not allowed access to prisoners held in NISS custody, however.

Christian clergy held services in prisons, but access was irregular and varied across prisons. Imams were granted access to facilitate Friday prayers.

There was no ombudsman or inspector general specifically designated for prisons. The police inspector general, the minister of justice, and the judiciary are authorized to inspect prisons.

<u>Independent Monitoring</u>: The government did not permit unrestricted monitoring by independent nongovernmental observers such as the International Committee of the Red Cross (ICRC). The ICRC was not allowed to visit prisons during the year and was required to get permits to travel to conflict areas. The majority of its work comprised tracing missing persons and reuniting families separated by conflict.

The government denied unrestricted access to diplomatic missions for consular visits. Diplomatic missions rarely were notified when nationals from their countries were arrested. When embassies were notified of arrests, representatives were allowed to speak to detainees' families and lawyers but never allowed to visit inmates. There was no access to NISS or military intelligence detention facilities.

The Ministry of Justice occasionally granted the UN Mission in Darfur (UNAMID) access to government prisons in Darfur, but with restrictions. The government in most cases denied access to specific files, records, and prisoners. As such, UNAMID was unable to verify inmates who reportedly were held illegally as political prisoners brought in by NISS, after having undergone no judicial process. The human rights section had unfettered physical access to general prisons (with the exception of NISS and Military Intelligence detention centers) in South, North, East, and West Darfur, but in Central Darfur (where most of the conflict occurred during the year), UNAMID had no access to any prison or detention center.

During the year the government granted the UN independent expert for the human rights situation in Sudan access to the Omdurman Men's and Women's Prisons, where he was briefed on detention conditions.

The state of detention facilities administered by Sudan Liberation Movement-- Abdul Wahid (SLM/AW) and Sudan People's Liberation Movement--North (SPLM-N) in their respective rebel-controlled areas could not be verified due to lack of access.

d. Arbitrary Arrest or Detention

The Interim National Constitution prohibits arbitrary arrest and detention and requires that individuals be notified of the charges against them when they are arrested. Arbitrary arrests and detentions, however, remained common under the law, which allows for arrest without warrants and detention up to four and one-half months. Authorities often released detainees when their initial detention periods expired but took them into custody the next day for an additional period.

Authorities, especially NISS, arbitrarily detained political opponents and those believed to sympathize with the opposition (see section 1.e.).

Role of the Police and Security Apparatus

Several government entities have responsibility for internal security, including the Ministries of Interior and Defense and NISS. The government attempted to respond to some interethnic fighting, and, in a few instances, was effective in mediating peaceful solutions. The government had a poor record, however, in preventing societal violence. Numerous residents in Darfur, for example, routinely complained of a lack of governing presence or authority that could prevent or deter violent crime.

NISS is responsible for internal security and all intelligence matters. It functions independent of any ministry. Constitutional amendments passed in January 2015 expanded NISS's mandate to include authorities traditionally reserved for the military and judiciary. Under the amendments, NISS may establish courts and is allowed greater latitude for making arrests; its officers are shielded from normal prosecution. The Ministry of Interior oversees the national police, including security police, Special Forces police, traffic police, and the combat-trained Central Reserve police. There was a police presence throughout the country. The Ministry of Defense oversees all elements of the SAF, including the Border Guards and military intelligence units.

In 2013 the government created the RSF, a new element of the security apparatus. A former SAF general commanded the RSF, but NISS oversaw its operations. The RSF continued to play a significant role in the government's campaigns against rebel movements and was implicated in the majority of reports of human rights violations against civilians. The government tightly controlled information about the RSF, and public comment critical of the RSF often resulted in arrest or detention (see section 2.a.). In June the president decided the RSF would report directly to him. In at least one case in October in White Nile State, the RSF clashed with SAF after the RSF caused a disturbance in a nearby settlement resulting in several casualties. Afterward, the SAF commander (not the RSF commander) was summoned to Khartoum for reprimand.

While the law provides NISS officials with legal protection for acts committed in their official capacity, the government reported NISS maintained an internal court system to address internal discipline and investigate and prosecute violations of the National Security Act, including abuse of power under the act. Penalties included up to 10 years in prison, a fine, or both for NISS officers found in violation. During the year, however, the government gave no access to information regarding how many cases it had closed. In October a key national dialogue recommendation was to rescind unilateral additions to the constitution that exempt NISS from the national jurisprudence system. Despite promises to implement all national dialogue recommendations, as of December the government did not include NISS reforms as part of the national dialogue package of laws it presented to the National Assembly.

NGOs reported that clashes between protesters and government forces in September 2013 caused more than 185 deaths (see section 1.a.). The government announced the Ministry of Justice would investigate the government's use of force. The government provided its conclusions to the UN independent expert on the situation of human rights in Sudan in 2014. Contrary to the independent expert's recommendations, the government did not make its full report public. Lawyers representing the affected families stated that most of the families did not want compensation but wanted apprehension and trial of the perpetrators. Lawyers stated that only a minority of families settled for compensation, and the government had not compensated any families who had opted for such compensation. Government officials asserted only 85 families were eligible for compensation. Of the 85 families, the government claimed it had already compensated 81. Opposition figures denied any compensation had been made and challenged the government to publish names of those who had been compensated, but the government refused.

Following a July visit to Darfur by a foreign government official, 15 Darfuri internally displaced persons (IDPs) who had spoken with him in Nertiti and Sortoni were arrested as was a UNAMID worker who had aided in arranging the meetings. By September, eight were released, including the UNAMID staff member; seven others remained detained and were transferred to a central location in Zalengei, Darfur. When pressed about these cases in August, Human Rights Advisory Council rapporteur Yassir Ahmed Alhassan stated that the council could not respond to every human rights abuse reported by media. By November, six more detainees had been released, and one remained in detention in Zalengei.

Corruption among police and other security forces continued to be a problem. Security forces including police harassed suspected government opponents. On June 1, the Ministry of Justice announced it had closed the case of the 2012 deaths of three students of al-Jazeera University. The general counselor reported the investigation confirmed the involvement of some police, and the prosecution ordered the lifting of their immunity as a step toward taking them to court. The ministry reportedly contacted the three students' families afterward and offered financial compensation of an unknown amount, which the three families reportedly accepted.

Impunity remained a serious problem throughout the security forces, although crimes involving child victims were prosecuted more regularly. Aside from the inconsistent use of NISS' special courts (see above), the government infrequently lifted police immunity or pressed charges against SAF officers. The government also generally failed to investigate violations committed by any branch of the security forces.

Arrest Procedures and Treatment of Detainees

Under the National Security Act, warrants are not required for an arrest. The law permits authorities to detain individuals for three days for the purpose of inquiry. The magistrate can renew detention without charge for up to two weeks. The superior magistrate may renew detentions weekly during investigation for up to six months for a person who is charged.

The law allows detentions for up to 45 days before individuals are charged. The NISS director may refer certain cases to the Security Council and request an extension of up to three months, allowing detentions of up to four and one-half months without charge. Authorities often released detainees when their detentions expired and rearrested them soon after for a new detention period, so that detainees were held for several months without charge.

The constitution and law provide for an individual to be informed in detail of charges at the time of arrest, with interpretation as needed, and for judicial determination without undue delay, but these provisions were rarely followed. Individuals accused of threatening national security routinely were charged under the national security law, rather than the criminal code, and frequently detained without charge.

The law allows for bail, except for those accused of crimes punishable by death or life imprisonment. There was a functioning bail system; however, the cases of persons released on bail often awaited action indefinitely.

The law provides for access to legal representation, but security forces often held persons incommunicado for long periods in unknown locations. By law, any person may request legal assistance and must be informed of the right to counsel in cases potentially involving the death penalty, imprisonment lasting longer than 10 years, or amputation. The government was not always able to provide legal assistance, and legal aid organizations and lawyers partially filled the gap.

Arbitrary Arrest: NISS, police, and military intelligence arbitrarily arrested and detained persons. Authorities often detained persons for a few days before releasing them without charge, but many persons were held much longer. The government often targeted political opponents and suspected rebel supporters (see section 1.e.).

NISS officials frequently denied holding individuals in their custody or refused to confirm their place of detention. In lieu of formal detention, NISS increasingly called individuals to report to NISS offices for long hours on a daily basis without a stated purpose. Many human rights observers considered this a tactic to harass, intimidate, and disrupt the lives of opposition members and activists, prevent the carrying out of "opposition" activities, and prevent the recording of formal detentions.

In November and December, hundreds of persons were detained without charges, including several prominent human rights activists and the leadership of registered political parties, some for weeks without visits from families or counsel. Most of the arrests were part of a general crackdown that followed calls for civil disobedience over government austerity measures. For example, NISS agents arrested prominent human rights activist Mudawi Ibrahim Adam on December 7. He remained in detention without charge at year's end.

Authorities also arbitrarily arrested and detained foreign nationals without charge. In some cases authorities used intimidation and financial pressure to force foreigners to leave the country.

The government sometimes sought to get Sudanese citizens living abroad deported from their countries of residence. In July 2015 Waleed al-Hussein, the creator of critical online news outlet *al-Rakoba*, was arrested in Saudi Arabia, where he had been residing with his family. He was subjected to interrogations about his work with *al-Rakoba*, held in solitary confinement without charge for more than two months, and threatened with deportation to Sudan. In November 2015 he was transferred to a general holding cell. Family members believed he was arrested at the request of the Sudanese government, which had targeted Hussein for his work in the past and was seeking to have him extradited to Sudan. The government, however, denied having anything to do with the journalist's detention. Al-Hussein was released from prison in March, but Saudi authorities did not give him an exit permit to depart Saudi Arabia until September.

There were reports of individuals detained due to their actual or assumed support of antigovernment forces, such as the Sudan People's Liberation Movement-North (SPLM-N) and Darfur rebel movements. Local NGOs reported that some women were detained because of their association with men suspected of being SPLM-N supporters (see section 1.g.).

Pretrial Detention: Lengthy pretrial detention was common. The large number of detainees and judicial inefficiency resulted in trial delays. In cases involving political defendants accused of subverting national security, the accused may be held for as long as four and one- half months, with the possibility of further extended detention periods, before being formally charged. In his report to the Human Rights Council, the UN independent expert on the situation of human rights in Sudan expressed concern about several reports received of prolonged detentions and persons held without access to legal aid. He called on the government to release all detained persons or charge them with a recognizable offense in accordance with the law.

A number of pastors arrested in December 2015 remained detained during the year. Some were released but required to report daily to NISS. In December 2015 Kowa Shamal, Hassan Abdelrahim, and Christian activist Talahon Nigosi Kassa Ratta were arrested. Yamani Abraha, Filmon Hassan, Ayoub Talian, and Yacoub Naway were arrested and released later the same day. NISS arrested Christian activists Peter Jasek (a Czech citizen), Ali Omer, and Abdelmoneim Abdelmaula in December 2015 in connection with the pastors. Shamal, Abdelrahim, Jasek, and Abdelmaula were held without charge until August, when they were charged with eight crimes, including espionage and warring against the state, crimes that carry the death penalty. As of year's end, all remained in custody and trials continued. In late December, Sudanese Church of Christ Pastor Kuwa Shamal was released after charges against him were dropped due to insufficient evidence.

Detainees' Ability to Challenge Lawfulness of Detention before a Court: Persons arrested or detained, regardless of whether on criminal or other grounds, were not entitled to challenge in court the legal basis or arbitrary nature of their detention and, therefore, were not able to obtain prompt release or compensation if unlawfully detained.

<u>Amnesty</u>: In September 2015 the government granted general amnesty for leaders and members of the armed movements taking part in the national dialogue. The amnesty covered "all words and deeds that constitute crimes during the period of the participation in the national dialogue." Many observers considered the amnesty a government incentive to encourage opposition members living abroad to return to the country for participation in the dialogue without fear of arrest or reprisal. As of November there were no known reports of arrests of opposition members who participated in the dialogue, although NISS detained and seized the travel documents of opposition members who met abroad (see section 2.d.). Leading opposition members living in exile who had called for more freedoms as a condition to their participation in the dialogue had not taken advantage of the general amnesty. The decree also called for the release of political prisoners whose parties participated in the dialogue. There were no known reports of such releases.

e. Denial of Fair Public Trial

Although the constitution and relevant laws provide for an independent judiciary, courts were largely subordinate to government officials and the security forces, particularly in cases of alleged crimes against the state. On occasion courts displayed a degree of independence. Political interference with the courts, however, was commonplace, and some high-ranking members of the judiciary held positions in the Ministry of Interior or other ministries in the executive branch.

The judiciary was inefficient and subject to corruption. In Darfur and other remote areas, judges were often absent from their posts, delaying trials.

A state of emergency in Darfur, Blue Nile, and Southern Kordofan allowed for arrest and detention without trial.

Trial Procedures

The constitution and law provide for a fair and public trial as well as a presumption of innocence; however, this provision was rarely respected. Trials are open to the public at the discretion of the judge. In cases of national security and offenses against the state, trials are usually closed. The law stipulates that the government is obligated to provide a lawyer for indigents in cases in which punishment might exceed 10 years' imprisonment or include execution. Accused persons may also request assistance through the legal aid department at the Ministry of Justice or the Sudanese Bar Association.

By law criminal defendants must be informed promptly of the charges against them at the time of their arrest and charged in detail and with interpretation as needed. Individuals arrested by NISS often were not informed of the reasons for their arrest.

Defendants generally have the right to present evidence and witnesses, be present in court, confront accusers, and have access to government-held evidence relevant to their cases. Some defendants reportedly did not receive legal counsel, and counsel in some cases could only advise the defendant and not address the court. Persons in remote areas and in areas of conflict generally did not have access to legal counsel. The government sometimes did not allow defense witnesses to testify.

Defendants have the right to appeal, except in military trials, where there is no appeal. Defendants were sometimes permitted time and facilities to prepare their defense, although in more political cases, charges could be disclosed with little warning and could change as the trial proceeded. Defendants in common criminal cases, such as theft, as well as in politicized cases were often compelled to confess guilt while in police custody through physical abuse and police intimidation of family members.

Lawyers wishing to practice are required to maintain membership in the government-controlled Sudanese Bar Association. The government continued to arrest and harass lawyers whom it considered political opponents.

Military trials, which sometimes were secret and brief, lacked procedural safeguards. For example, a defendant's attorney could advise the defendant but could not address the court.

A 2013 amendment to the 2007 Sudanese Armed Forces Act subjects any civilians in SAF-controlled areas believed to be rebels or members of paramilitary group to military trials. NISS and military intelligence officers applied this amendment to detainees in the conflict areas. In 2013, SPLM-N forces attacked and captured Abu Karshola, South Kordofan. The government launched an intensive campaign to liberate Abu Karshola from the SPLM-N. Afterwards, seven civilians who supported SPLM-N were arrested and charged in a military court with treason and waging war against the state, which carries the death penalty. The court-martial concluded in June; charges against one defendant were dropped, and the remaining six awaited the final verdict as of September.

Three-person security courts deal with violations of constitutional decrees, emergency regulations, and some sections of the penal code, including drug and currency offenses. Special courts composed primarily of civilian judges handled most security-related cases. Defendants had limited opportunities to meet with counsel and were not always allowed to present witnesses during trial.

Due to long distances between court facilities and police stations, local mediation was often the first resort to try to resolve disputes. In some instances tribal courts operating outside the official legal system decided cases. Such courts did not provide the same protections as regular courts.

While Islamic jurisprudence (sharia) strongly influenced the law, sharia was generally not applied to Christians in civil domestic cases such as those concerning marriage, divorce, inheritance, and other family matters.

Political Prisoners and Detainees

The government continued to hold political prisoners and detainees, including protesters. Due to lack of access, the numbers of political prisoners and detainees could not be confirmed. Human rights monitors reported political prisoners as being in the hundreds; the government claimed it did not have political prisoners.

The government severely restricted international humanitarian organizations' and human rights monitors' access to political detainees. The government allowed UNAMID extremely limited access to Darfuri political detainees in Khartoum and Darfur.

The government also arbitrarily detained and otherwise targeted numerous Darfuri students on university campuses. On June 28, the Criminal Court in Khartoum North locality sentenced Ahmed Baggari to death by hanging in April, following legal proceedings after Baggari was accused of the April 2015 killing of Mohamed Awadelkarim, a fellow student and the secretary general of the ruling NCP Party-aligned Islamic Movement in East Nile College in Khartoum. Baggari's defense team appealed the case to the Court of Appeals. In December the Court of Appeals cancelled the death sentence and ordered his imprisonment for five years and a payment of SDG 40,000 ($6,000) in compensation to the relatives of Awadelkarim.

Government authorities detained Darfuri students and political opponents throughout the year, often subjecting them to torture (see section 1.c.).

The government continued to arrest or temporarily detain opposition members. In November, following the government's announcement of fuel subsidy cuts, NISS "preventatively" detained 29 political opposition leaders, primarily from the Sudanese Congress Party (SCoP), the Communist Party, and the National Consensus Forces. There were numerous examples similar to the following: On November 27, NISS agents followed the vehicle of Dr. Galal Yousif, a member of the SCoP, before intimidating, forcefully abducting, and taking him to an unknown location. As of December, Yousif remained in detention without access to his family or his lawyer.

In April authorities detained more than 25 University of Khartoum graduates after they participated in a protest against the reported selling of the university's main campus. Numerous university students were also arrested and released in May and again detained after a raid on their lawyer's office (see sections 1.b. and 1.f.). The length of their detentions varied.

Civil Judicial Procedures and Remedies

Persons seeking damages for human rights violations had access to domestic and international courts. The judiciary, however, was not independent. There were problems enforcing domestic and international court orders (see section 5). According to the law, individuals and organizations may appeal adverse domestic decisions to regional human rights bodies. Individuals, however, reported they feared reprisal (see section 2.d.).

f. Arbitrary or Unlawful Interference with Privacy, Family, Home, or Correspondence

The Interim National Constitution and law prohibit such actions, but the government routinely violated these rights. Emergency laws in Darfur, Southern Kordofan, and Blue Nile states legalize interference in privacy, family, home, and correspondence.

Security forces frequently conducted searches without warrants and targeted persons suspected of political crimes. NISS often confiscated private property, especially electronic equipment. During a May raid on the legal office and home of prominent human rights lawyer Nabil Adeeb, NISS agents entered without judicial authorization and confiscated Adeeb's personal laptop, hardcopy files, and mobile phone. The authorities never returned Adeeb's laptop and files, although they returned his mobile phone shortly afterward.

The government monitored private communication and movement of individuals and organizations without due legal process. A wide network of government informants conducted surveillance in schools, universities, markets, workplaces, and neighborhoods.

Under sharia a Muslim man may marry a Jewish or Christian woman. A Muslim woman may not marry a non-Muslim man. This prohibition was not universally enforced. Non-Muslims may adopt only non-Muslim children; a comparable restriction does not apply to Muslim parents.

In May 2014 a local court sentenced Meriam Yahia Ibrahim Ishag to 100 lashes and death by hanging for committing apostasy and adultery by marrying a Christian man. Ishag identified herself as a Christian. The government released Ishag from custody in June 2014 after the Court of Appeals overturned her conviction, citing mental health issues. Following significant international pressure, authorities allowed her to leave the country the following month but did not officially rescind the charges against her. In December 2015 Ishag's defense panel appealed the court decision to the Constitutional Court in an effort to challenge the constitutionality of apostasy. As of September the case remained pending.

g. Abuses in Internal Conflict

<u>Killings</u>: From January to September, military personnel and paramilitary forces committed numerous killings in Darfur and the Two Areas. In mid-January the government launched an aerial and ground offensive to dislodge the SLA/AW from its strongholds in the mountainous areas of Central, North, and South Darfur.

According to press and NGO reports, RSF personnel under NISS command committed numerous killings, often after barrel bombs were dropped by Antonov An-26 aircraft during government offensives in Darfur and the Two Areas. Human rights groups reported such aerial bombardments disproportionately hurt civilians. Most reports were difficult to verify due to continued prohibited access to conflict areas, particularly Jebel Marra in Darfur and SPLM-N-controlled areas in South Kordofan and Blue Nile States.

In late September, Amnesty International issued a report alleging that, during the first nine months of the year, the government engaged in scorched earth tactics and used chemical weapons in Jebel Marra, Darfur, resulting in deaths. UN monitors were unable to verify the alleged use of chemical weapons, due in part to the lack of access to Jebel Marra from rebel commanders loyal to Abdel Wahid. At year's end the OPCW had not been presented with sufficient corroborating evidence to conclude chemical weapons had been used.

Clashes between government forces, government-armed militias, and rebel movements, notably the SLA/AW in Darfur and the SPLM-N in the Two Areas, resulted in casualties on all sides. Sudan Liberation Army/Minni Minawi and Justice and Equality Movement/Gibril were generally inactive during the year. Intercommunal conflict and societal violence continued to be the most deadly consequences of the conflict in Darfur. The continued utilization and arming of local militias as proxies and the continued influence of these groups in part due to their heavy armament, coupled with widespread impunity, allowed the conflict to spread systemically as clashes over land, cattle, and other resources intensified. Clashes between heavily armed communal groups, particularly in East, South, and North Darfur, resulted in significant casualties (dead and injured) on all sides.

Many deaths continued to be attributed to the SAF and militia groups. Security deteriorated in North Darfur. Violence in the Jebel Marra area of East Darfur, including indiscriminate SAF aerial and artillery bombardments, continued, although this largely ceased by September.

On May 1, the SAF bombed Heiban, South Kordofan, killing six children. The incident drew widespread protests in Khartoum following the sharing of their pictures via social media. On May 23, during the memorial service for the six children, an SAF jet dropped two bombs in the area, injuring four more children and killing a six-month-old baby. On May 27, two parachute bombs were dropped onto the compound of St. Vincent Primary School in Kauda, injuring a Kenyan teacher and damaging classrooms and a library. Casualties were limited, as the attack did not take place during school hours. Reports of such aerial attacks in South Kordofan and Blue Nile State ceased by September.

SAF air raids resulted in civilian deaths and the destruction of fields and impeded the planting of crops throughout Darfur and the Two Areas. Throughout the year the SAF repeatedly bombed cultivated land, disrupting planting cycles, which, coupled with forced displacements and the denial of humanitarian assistance, resulted in near famine-like conditions. There were also numerous reports of the

SAF using cluster bombs in both Darfur and the Two Areas. NGOs accused the government of using the denial of food as a weapon of war.

On June 9, ICC prosecutor Fatou Bensouda reported to the UN Security Council that aerial bombardments had resulted in more than 400 civilian deaths and up to 200 villages destroyed. She also reported that air raids on January 21 on an East Jebel Marra village reportedly killed 48 women and destroyed six houses. The UN Security Council's Panel of Experts on Darfur stated it had evidence the country's air force had RBK-500 cluster bombs at the weapon-loading area at the Nyala Forward Operation Base. On March 25, the SAF shelled al-Habel village in Um Dorein County of South Kordofan and injured two girls, 11 and 10 years old.

In April, SAF raids killed five children and injured 22. Multiple schools were reportedly bombed and others closed due to the fighting, particularly those near the front line. The Sudan Social Development Organization (SUDO UK), a UK-based human rights monitoring organization with sources on the ground in conflict areas, also reported that aerial bombardments in Darfur and the Two Areas killed 391 persons and injured 417. Various reports corroborated a minimum of seven aerial bombardments in Darfur in August alone, focused on the Jebel Marra region, Central Darfur, with two raids in North Darfur and one in South Darfur. There were numerous abuses similar to the following example: On August 29, in the North Darfur village of Kator, government-aligned militias attacked a group of displaced civilians, killing three and injuring four. The IDP's were fleeing earlier bombardments on their home village of Qabas.

In Darfur clashes between the government and rebel factions continued, as did attacks by the government's RSF forces on unarmed civilians in South, North, and East Darfur and in the Two Areas.

Ground attacks targeting civilians were also serious problems in both Darfur and the Two Areas. There were numerous abuses similar to the following example: On June 12, an SAF soldier shot and killed Amna Adam Kuku in Elfaid Um-Abdalla because he reportedly suspected her brother was a sympathizer of the SPLM-N.

The following incident involving NISS is illustrative of abuses taking place in West Darfur: On January 8, the body of a shepherd for the Arab Bani Halba tribe was found near the Massalit village of Moli, approximately six to 12 miles south of El Geneina. According to UNAMID, the Bani Halba demanded compensation, but the Massalit denied involvement and refused. On January 9, Bani Halba tribesmen, many or all of whom served as border guards--supported by fellow border guards from the Arab tribes of Maharia, Awlad Janoub, Awlad Marni, and Sheigerat--attacked Moli with up to 200 men and 20 Toyota Land Cruisers in retaliation. Reportedly five to 10 Massalit were killed, and many IDPs fled to El Geneina. On January 10, the displaced Massalit from Moli protested in front of the governor's offices. Protests reportedly turned violent when no one acknowledged their complaints. The demonstrators forcefully entered the governor's office and residence, set afire a tent and offices (reportedly the residence of the governor's security guards), and burned or upended multiple vehicles.

The protesters put up barricades of burning tires in front of the governor's compound. Police and NISS subsequently clashed with the protesters and opened fire with live ammunition, killing six. There were also unconfirmed reports that either Arab tribesmen or Massalit protesters killed a NISS officer during the protests, taking his weapon, in addition to seven to eight NISS officers injured. On January 11, while Massalit protesters were still occupying the governor's compound (although confrontation had ceased), shots were fired into the funeral procession of those who were killed on January 10, killing at least three additional Massalit IDPs and wounding six others. The shots were reportedly fired while the procession was passing NISS offices, and reportedly security forces had mistaken the large group of mourners for protesters. In all, at least 13 persons were killed, while many more were wounded.

There were also numerous abuses of detainees reported similar to the following: On February 16, NISS in Tadamoun locality arrested Elnour Mohammed Elfadeel at his house following accusations he possessed a gun without a license. On February 17, he arrived at Damazine Military Hospital in critical condition and died in the hospital that same day. Medical sources stated the cause of death was fractures to the neck and skull.

According to the ICC prosecutor's June report, in both Darfur and the Two Areas, there were reported attacks on humanitarian aid workers and peacekeepers, with one peacekeeper killed in Darfur.

In Abyei, the security situation remained unpredictable but generally calm. Most human rights abuses were due to tribal conflict between the Ngok Dinka and Misseriya, with several major security incidents occurring in and around the marketplaces. On May 8, UN Interim Security Force in Abyei (UNISFA) troops disarmed a Misseriya and an Ngok Dinka found with a rifle and hand grenade, respectively, at the Noong common market. On June 21, in the Kolom area, unknown assailants armed with automatic rifles and rocket-propelled grenades opened fire on a commercial pickup vehicle transporting traders from Twic County in Warrap State, South Sudan, to the common market at Noong. The attack left three persons dead and two seriously wounded. On June 21, UNISFA reported that unknown armed men shot at a civilian vehicle with seven persons on board travelling from Agok to Noog, Abyei, killing three persons and injuring two others.

Abductions: International organizations were unable independently to verify reports of disappearances due to lack of access to the region. Humanitarian actors reported unverified cases of government-aligned forces abducting or detaining civilians, including women, due to their suspected affiliation with the SPLM-N.

There were numerous abuses similar to the following: According to the Human Rights and Development Organization, a monitoring organization with sources on the ground in the Two Areas, Musa Aabdein Ali, a government employee, was found alive but in poor health in military intelligence custody on March 15 after five years of detention. He was abducted in 2011 soon after hostilities erupted in South Kordofan. Ali reportedly had no political affiliation. Military intelligence, NISS, and political authorities denied knowing his whereabouts. Ali reported he was detained incommunicado and faced physical abuse and poor health and sanitary conditions.

SUDO UK reported 86 abductions throughout the conflict areas from January to August, 45 in May alone. UNAMID reported 55 abductions in Darfur from January to September 15. While government or government-aligned entities perpetrated the majority of these abductions, some were carried out by unknown armed criminal groups. One such incident in January included a carjacking, two robberies, and the abduction of a World Food Program (WFP)-contract driver and his truck. The driver was released in the Kutum area several days later.

UNAMID reported that abduction remained a coercive method adopted by the various tribes in Darfur to obtain the payment of *diya* ("blood money" ransom) claimed from other communities.

Physical Abuse, Punishment, and Torture: Human rights organizations accused government forces and rebel groups in Darfur and the Two Areas of perpetrating torture and other human rights violations and abuses. Government forces abused persons detained in connection with armed conflict as well as IDPs suspected of having links to rebel groups. There were continuing reports that government security forces, progovernment and antigovernment militias, and other armed persons raped women and children.

In Darfur, fighting involved government forces, rebels, and ethnic militias, and it was often along communal lines. These armed groups, including the RSF, which NISS controlled, killed and injured civilians, raped women and children, looted properties, targeted IDP camps, and burned villages in all of Darfur's five states. Multiple sources reported the RSF also destroyed and plundered water wells, food stores, and community resources, including livestock. A September Amnesty International report alleged the government used chemical weapons to target civilian areas in Jebel Marra, Darfur from January to September. UN monitors were unable to verify the alleged use of chemical weapons, due in part to lack of access to Jebel Marra and insufficient corroborating evidence. The report that also alleged the government engaged in scorched earth tactics was corroborated by multiple sources from Darfur.

These acts resulted in approximately 80,600 newly displaced persons by September, but, nevertheless, a decrease from 243,000 reported during the same period the previous year. An increase in criminality and banditry also contributed to a deterioration of overall security in Darfur. UNAMID continued to document hundreds of cases of human rights abuses, including unlawful killings, other abuses of the right to physical integrity, and arbitrary arrest and detention.

Sexual and gender-based violence continued throughout Darfur and the Two Areas. The ICC prosecutor in her June report to the UN Security Council noted 107 reported incidents of sexual crimes affecting 225 victims, indicating that 70 per cent of these incidents involved gang rape, of which 19 per cent victimized minors. Authorities often obstructed access to justice for rape victims. IDPs reported perpetrators of such violence were often government armed force or militia members. SUDO UK reported the confirmed rape by RSF agents of 125 persons, mostly IDP's, including 32 minors, from January to August in both Darfur and the Two Areas.

Widespread impunity remained a major challenge, aggravated by government's limited capacity, the absence of a security environment conducive to civilian safety across Darfur, and use of excess force by security forces. For example, on March 24, NISS agents reportedly arrested a female student on her way to the University of El Geneina and assaulted her. Seven students from Nyala University who were arrested on April 26 for demonstrating against the increase in public transport fees reported having been similarly beaten in detention. Neither case had been investigated by year's end.

The government prosecuted some crimes involving government officials. Although rare, prosecutions were most common in cases involving violations against minors. On May 10, a court in El Geneina convicted and sentenced a soldier to 20 years' imprisonment for the rape of a seven-year-old girl. The UN Independent Expert for the human rights situation in Sudan expressed concern about nine rapes of women from the Zam camp in April, when they were outside the camp engaged in livelihood activities.

The SAF and government-aligned forces also reportedly burned and looted villages in Southern Kordofan and Blue Nile. There were reports of physical abuse and violent interrogations of SPLM-N-affiliated individuals in Kadugli Prison and military installations.

Human rights groups continued to report that government forces and allied militias raped, detained, tortured, and arbitrarily killed civilians in government-controlled areas of Blue Nile. SUDO UK reported 269 cases of arbitrary arrest, 56 of which involved civilians detained in containers in Damazine, Blue Nile.

On March 31, Radio Tamazuj reported shelling by the SPLM-N of civilian areas in Kadugli town, specifically Sama, Saraf, and Um Bataha neighborhoods. Reported claims by "local sources" that "nobody was hurt" were difficult to verify.

In July and August, the government accused the SPLM-N of attacking a Chinese-run gold mine bordering South and North Kordofan. The attacks were difficult to verify due to lack of access.

There were varying reports in July of violence that affected civilians in Lima, Southern Kordofan, including reports that eight Misseriya tribesmen were killed during an altercation with an SPLM-N soldier over a reported cattle theft. It was unclear, however, whether the Misseriya killed were civilians or part of the government-aligned militia Popular Defense Forces.

Unexploded ordinance killed and injured many innocent civilians in the country's conflict zones. There were numerous examples similar to the following: On November 27, in Singa, north of Damazine, Blue Nile, the explosion of an undetonated remnant of war injured five children.

On March 27, the *Radio Dabanga* online newspaper reported six gold miners died in an explosion in Tawila locality of Darfur when their vehicle drove over and detonated unexploded ordinance. Apart from the six miners who were killed, three others were reportedly seriously injured.

Child Soldiers: The law prohibits the recruitment of children and provides criminal penalties for perpetrators. Allegations persisted, however, that armed movements, government forces, and government-aligned militias had child soldiers within their ranks.

According to several reports, the government provided material and logistical support in the country to the South Sudan opposition group, Sudan People's Liberation Army in Opposition, which was widely reported to recruit and use child soldiers.

Many children lacked documents verifying their age. Children's rights organizations believed armed groups exploited this lack of documentation to recruit or retain children. Due to problems of access, particularly in conflict zones, reports of child soldiers were limited and often difficult to verify. The government denied allegations it recruited or used child soldiers within its armed forces. During the March 27 to 30 visit of the UN special representative for children and armed conflict, the government signed an action plan to end and prevent recruitment and use of children by its security forces. The special representative documented 21 children detained by NISS since April and August 2015 for their alleged association with the rebel group JEM. The children had allegedly been recruited in South Kordofan and South Sudan and used in combat in Darfur and South Sudan. In September the government pardoned and released the children to a reintegration program. JEM representatives claimed the children did not belong to their faction. In addition, the United Nations documented the recruitment of six children by JEM from refugee settlements in Unity State, South Sudan. In September the country's Disarmament, Demobilization, and Reintegration (DDR) Commission reported that 169 child soldiers, all from the Liberation and Justice Movement, had been assembled in South Darfur for DDR procedures.

In September, UNAMID reported that concerted efforts to curb the recruitment of child soldiers in Darfur had led to significant progress, but the potential use of children in ethnic clashes remained a major concern.

Representatives of armed groups reported they did not actively recruit child soldiers. They did not prevent children who volunteered from joining their movements. The armed groups stated the children were stationed primarily in training camps and were not used in combat.

There were reports of the use of child soldiers by the SPLM-N, but numbers could not be verified, in part due to lack of access to SPLM-N-controlled territories. On November 23, in Geneva, Malik Agar of the SPLM-N and Leila Zerrougui, the representative of the UN secretary-general on children and armed conflict, signed an action plan to end the recruitment and use of child soldiers. In her remarks, Zerrougui said the government, nonstate actors, and everyone involved in armed conflict must cooperate and acknowledge that the rules of law "apply to children two times over." She noted that Sudan ratified the Convention on the Rights of the Child in 1990 and is party to other international agreements, meaning the legal framework is in place and the main focus should be implementation.

Also see the Department of State's *Trafficking in Persons Report* at www.state.gov/j/tip/rls/tiprpt/.

Other Conflict-related Abuse: All parties to the conflict in Darfur obstructed the work of humanitarian organizations, UNAMID, and other UN agencies, increasing the displacement of civilians and abuse of IDPs. The government also continued to deny access to humanitarian organizations and UN agencies in Darfur, the Jebel Marra region in particular, and all government-controlled areas of Southern Kordofan and Blue Nile (the SPLM-N also denied access to areas in their control), isolating an estimated 800,000 IDPs and severely limiting access to life-saving humanitarian assistance. Violence, insecurity, the delay and denial of visas and travel permits, and refusal of access to international organizations reduced the ability of humanitarian organizations to provide needed services. As of December 20, 30 visas requested in January by UNAMID remained pending.

Government forces frequently harassed NGOs that received international assistance. The government restricted or denied permission for humanitarian assessments, refused to approve technical agreements, changed operational procedures, copied NGO files, confiscated NGO property, questioned humanitarian workers at length and monitored their personal correspondence, restricted travel, and publicly accused humanitarian workers of aiding rebel groups. Unidentified armed groups also targeted humanitarian workers for kidnapping and ransom.

Fighting, insecurity, bureaucratic obstacles, and government and rebel restrictions reduced the ability of peacekeepers and humanitarian workers to access conflict-affected areas. Armed persons attacked, killed, injured, and kidnapped peacekeepers and aid workers. Humanitarian organizations often were not able to deliver humanitarian assistance in conflict areas, particularly in Jebel Marra, South Darfur. According to the UN secretary-general's report on UNAMID on March 22, the SLA/AW faction attacked UNAMID forces with heavy weapons near Kutum on January 1, injuring one South African peacekeeper. In November armed men abducted three staffers of the Office of the UN High Commissioner for Refugees (UNHCR): two Nepalese and one a Sudanese national. During the same week, five armed masked men in a Land Cruiser without license plates abducted three Sudanese employees of UNAMID in Nyala, the capital of South Darfur, while they were traveling to the mission's headquarters, which is 13 miles southeast of Nyala.

All states in Darfur were under varying states of emergency. Between December 2015 and September, there were 1,626 cases of criminality and banditry, which included 384 killings. The attacks included rape, armed robbery, abduction, ambush, livestock theft, assault/harassment, arson, and burglary and were allegedly carried out primarily by Arab militias, but also by government forces, unknown assailants, and rebel elements.

Security in Darfur continued to deteriorate due to the rise in criminal activity and intercommunal conflict. The independent expert on the situation of human rights in Sudan noted with concern that, during the year, the size and scale of intercommunal clashes over cattle rustling and control of natural resources in Eastern Darfur had been unprecedented, as were the sophisticated firearms used by the combatants.

Large-scale displacement continued to be a severe problem in Darfur and the Two Areas, and government restrictions and security constraints continued to limit access to affected populations and impeded the delivery of humanitarian services (see section 2.d.).

Throughout the year the Humanitarian Aid Commission (HAC) obstructed the work of NGOs and international humanitarian actors in the country's conflict zones (see section 5).

Following meetings between UNAMID and the government, food-ration containers were released from Port Sudan, while, as of September, 59 shipments (101 containers) were still pending clearance. A total of 367 shipments of UN-owned and contingent-owned equipment, some of which had been there since April 2015, remained at Port Sudan and Khartoum, pending Ministry of Finance approval and customs clearance. The resulting shortages severely hampered the ability of UNAMID troops to communicate, conduct robust patrols, and protect civilians; they incurred demurrage charges and additional costs for troop- and police-contributing countries and the United Nations.

Attacks on humanitarian and UNAMID convoys continued. Bandits obstructed humanitarian assistance, regularly attacked the compounds of humanitarian organizations, and seized humanitarian aid and other assets, including vehicles. Instability forced many international aid organizations to reduce their operations in Darfur. The UN secretary-general stated, however, that the number of attacks against UN agencies and humanitarian organizations continued to decline. On March 27, a national staff member of the WFP was robbed in Nyala, South Darfur. On April 5, three local staff members of an international nongovernmental organization were robbed near El Geneina, West Darfur. Humanitarian organizations regularly reported encountering challenges in their humanitarian action and protection activities owing to access restrictions, interference with program administration and implementation by authorities, and the negative effects of continuing hostilities and incidents of violence and intimidation.

There were several reports of government forces, and armed militias and individuals, raiding IDP camps. On April 18, IDPs at the North camp, Central Darfur, reported that authorities had instructed them not to release any information to UNAMID. Moreover, the government did not allow civil society groups operating health-care centers to deal with cases involving conflict-related sexual and gender-based violence, especially in Central Darfur.

Largely unregulated artisanal gold-mining activities continued to expand in all of the Darfur states and to be a source of tension between communities. Claims to land rights continued to be mostly ethnic and tribal in nature. Clashes sometimes resulted from conflicts over land rights, mineral ownership, and use of gold-mining areas, particularly in the Jebel Amer area in North Darfur. Observers believed those clashes resulted in significant numbers of deaths and displacement.

Although the government made public statements encouraging the return of IDPs to their homes and the closure of camps in Darfur since "peace" had come to Darfur, IDPs expressed reluctance to return due to lack of security and justice in their areas of origin or elsewhere.

In the Two Areas there continued to be reports that SAF air raids destroyed homes, schools, churches, mosques, other civilian structures, and farms, and that humanitarian aid workers and centers, including hospitals, were targeted (see section 1.g.).

Restrictions imposed by the government in Abyei on NGOs limited the implementation capacity of humanitarian and development actors, especially in the northern parts of Abyei. Additional problems included inadequate funds, high implementation costs owing to security and logistical constraints, delays in the issuance of travel permits, and government restrictions on the movement of personnel and supplies.

The United Nations reported that during the year it received two allegations of sexual exploitation and abuse by a civilian and by a UN volunteer deployed to UNISFA. One incident allegedly took place in 2015; the date of the other alleged incident was unknown. Because the allegations were against a UN civilian staff member and volunteer, the United Nations did not provide the nationalities of the accused. Both allegations were being investigated by the United Nations at year's end.

UNISFA regularly conducted sensitization and awareness raising activities with staff members of all components. UN personnel carried out similar campaigns with the local population during which they highlighted and explained the UN policy on zero tolerance of sexual exploitation and abuse by UN personnel.

Section 2. Respect for Civil Liberties, Including:

a. Freedom of Speech and Press

The Interim National Constitution provides for freedom of thought, expression, and of the press "as regulated by law," but the government heavily restricted these rights.

<u>Freedom of Speech and Expression</u>: Individuals who criticized the government publicly or privately were subject to reprisal, including arrest. The government attempted to impede such criticism and monitored political meetings and the press. In July the government arrested Imam Yousif Abdullah Abaker following an Eid al-Fitr sermon in Aljenina in West Darfur, during which he criticized the central and state governments and blamed them for deaths in Darfur and throughout the country. He was reportedly transferred to Khartoum and sentenced to nine months in prison.

In March, NISS summoned and interrogated Rokaya al-Zaki, a journalist at *al-Ray al-Aam* newspaper, after publication of a financial corruption article relating to the Workers' Union. NISS confiscated the independent daily *al-Jarida's* press runs for unknown reasons on May 9, 10, 12, 13, and 16. In addition, journalists reported that security officers interrogated and harassed them. In November there were almost daily suspensions or confiscations of newspapers and radio stations by NISS for reporting on the nationwide civil disobedience that took place November 27 to 29 following the announcement of new austerity measures. Similarly, NISS seized newspapers on an almost daily basis throughout December, amid calls for large-scale protests. For example, NISS seized copies of daily *al-Tayyar* at least five times in December.

Throughout the year, more than 16 journalists were arrested, nine were subjected to legal actions against them by the government, at least 14 were summoned by NISS, and more than seven were suspended at some point. Throughout the year NISS detained more than 41 opposition party members, in some cases following meetings or symposiums during which attendees discussed politics.

The government also curtailed public discussion of a religious nature if proselytization was suspected and monitored religious sermons and teachings (see the Department of State's *International Religious Freedom Report* at www.state.gov/religiousfreedomreport/).

Press and Media Freedoms: The Interim National Constitution provides for freedom of the press, but authorities prevented newspapers from reporting on problems deemed sensitive. In December 2015 President Bashir 2015 criticized his government's inability to "control the media" in an address to the ruling NCP parliamentary caucus. He warned that he personally would take "decisive measures." Those measures included regular and direct prepublication censorship, confiscation of publications, legal proceedings, and denial of state advertising. Confiscation in particular inflicted financial damage on newspapers already under financial strain due to low circulation. The government verbally ordered newspapers throughout the year about "red line" topics on which the press could not report. Such topics included corruption, university protests, the national dialogue, political negotiations in Addis Ababa, the conflict in South Sudan, the doctors' nationwide strike, the weak economy and declining value of the Sudanese pound, power outages, outbreak of cholera, the security services, and government action in conflict areas. Authorities ordered the confiscation of newspapers that reported on these topics.

The government influenced radio and television reporting through the granting or denial of permits, as well as offering or withholding government payments for advertisements, based on how closely affiliated they were with the government.

On November 27, authorities issued a cease-and-desist order, closing indefinitely the privately owned satellite television channel Omdurman TV, which until then had seemed to be progovernment. According to its owner, the move likely came after a talk show the station aired in which ruling NCP party members discussed corruption as one of the possible factors in the country's continuing budget crisis. The government, however, claimed that the channel's license had expired.

The government controlled the media through the National Council for Press and Publications (NCPP), which administered mandatory professional examinations for journalists and oversaw the selection of editors. The NCPP had authority to ban journalists temporarily or indefinitely. In November the NCPP estimated there were 4,000 registered journalists in the country, a significant decrease from 7,000 in 2015. The council stated that registration of journalists was now handled primarily by the Sudanese Journalists Union, which may have more journalists on file with their organization. Of the 4,000 registered journalists in the country, approximately 600 were actively employed.

During the year authorities lifted restrictions on one journalist who had been temporarily banned from writing. As of December 2015, seven other journalists remained banned from writing, including four journalists for *al-Jarida* newspaper. As of November NISS had banned at least 16 journalists from publishing articles or suspended their newspapers from publishing.

<u>Violence and Harassment</u>: The government, including NISS, continued to arrest, harass, intimidate, and abuse journalists and vocal critics of the government. NISS required journalists to provide personal information, such as details on their tribe, political affiliation, and family.

According to Journalists for Human Rights, in early November NISS beat and arrested Mohamed al-Amin Abdel-Aziz, a journalist collaborator of *al-Jarida* newspaper. Also in early November, NISS allegedly beat and detained journalist Amal Habani after she left the premises of a courtroom in Khartoum where she attended the trial of several civil society activists. In December, NISS agents also arrested and allegedly beat a number of journalists, amid calls for large-scale protests against the lifting of fuel subsidies.

In late December 2015, lawyers referred to the Constitutional Court the case of Osman Mirghani, editor and chief of *al-Tayar* newspaper, who was attacked by unknown assailants in 2014 and whose newspaper's publication had been suspended as of December 2015. Some human rights advocates suspected the government instructed the court to delay its ruling. On May 1, the Constitutional Court issued an order allowing *al-Tayar* to resume publishing after more than four months of "indefinite suspension" by NISS (without compensation) and following a hunger strike/protest by the staff of the newspaper, in which other journalists and activists also participated. After its reopening, NISS continued to intimidate and harass *al-Tayar*, and confiscated print runs of the daily on a regular basis.

On July 27, *al-Tagheer* newspaper suspended its own publishing indefinitely following multiple consecutive confiscations.

On September 14, the Press and Publications Council ordered suspension of four newspapers (*Ilaf, al-Mostagil, al-Watan,* and *Awal al-Nahar*).

In January 2015 the Ministry of Culture revoked the Sudanese Writers Union's registration. The union had been registered since 2006 to hold intellectual forums, cultural nights, movie screenings, and other activities. The union filed a case against the Ministry of Culture. In October 2015 a judge ruled in favor of the union, disallowing justifications used by the ministry to close the group. In late 2015, however, the court reversed its judgment. The group was reportedly able to reregister on December 1.

Censorship or Content Restrictions: The government continued to practice direct prepublication and prebroadcast censorship of all forms of media. The government increased confiscations during the May aftermath of April protests by students that were sparked by reports of the government's alleged sale of the University of Khartoum to foreign investors. During the protests two students were killed, many were injured, and many were arrested. Confiscations of print runs was the censorship method most frequently used by NISS, having utility in terms of censoring material, incentivizing future self-censorship, and causing high financial losses to the publisher that could lead to the newspaper's eventual closure.

In 2014 the government announced it would suspend exceptional measures, including prepublication censorship, imposed by NISS on print media; however, such censorship continued unabated. According to the National Council for Press and Publications, in November 2015 a court specializing in media issues and "newspaper irregularities" was established under the existing Press and Publications Act. By August the Press and Publications Court was functional.

The government confiscated print runs of at least 12 newspapers on at least 49 occasions between March and November, mostly in May, following the widespread April student protests and in November following nationwide civil disobedience strikes and protests in response to government austerity measures. For example, in one week from November 25 to December 2, NISS confiscated 16 print runs of nine newspapers.

On November 30, the Sudan Journalist Network organized a one-day strike to protest the confiscations of print runs of five dailies (*al-Tayar*, *al-Watan*, *al-Jarida*, *al-Yom al-Taali*, and *al-Ayaam)* for four days in a row, from November 28 to December 1. Local journalists suspected the seizures were for publishing articles critical of the subsidy cuts made by the government on November 3. More than 100 independent journalists participated in the strike.

National Security: The Press and Publications Act allows for restrictions on the press in the interest of national security and public order. It contains loosely defined provisions for bans for encouraging ethnic and religious disturbances and incitement of violence. The act holds editors in chief criminally liable for all content published in their newspapers. The criminal code, National Security Act, and emergency laws were regularly used to bring charges against the press.

NISS initiated and continued legal action against journalists for stories critical of the government and security services.

In February, Ibrahim Baggal, a digital journalist and online activist, was arrested for criticizing the governor of North Darfur in a Facebook post and charged under the Information Technology (IT) Crime Act. Baggal spent 55 days in detention before his release on bail, but he was reportedly detained again days later and held for another week, for seemingly arbitrary reasons. The public prosecutor later dropped some of the charges against Baggal, namely undermining the constitutional order, waging war against the state, and contempt for authority; however, Baggal still faced charges of spreading false information, disclosing military information, and breaching public safety.

In Khartoum the state health minister also took legal action against *al-Watan* after the newspaper accused the minister of misappropriating public funds to enhance al-

Zaitona Hospital, one of three hospitals privately owned by the state health minister.

Internet Freedom

The government regulated licensing of telecommunications companies through the National Telecommunications Corporation. The agency blocked some websites and most proxy servers judged offensive to public morality, such as those purveying pornography. There were few restrictions on access to information websites, but authorities sporadically blocked access to YouTube and "negative" media sites. According to the International Telecommunication Union, approximately 27 percent of individuals used the internet in 2015, an increase from 25 percent in 2014.

Reporters without Borders reported NISS established a cyber-jihadist unit with a mandate to crack down on "internet dissidents" in 2011. According to outside reports, the unit continued to monitor social media accounts and electronic communications, especially of those believed to be regime critics.

Freedom House continued to rank the country as "not free" in its annual internet freedom report. According to the report, arrests and prosecutions under the IT Crime Act grew during the year, reflecting a tactical shift in the government's strategy to limit internet freedom. The report noted that many journalists writing for online platforms published anonymously to avoid prosecution, while ordinary internet users in the country had become more inclined to self-censor to avoid government surveillance and arbitrary legal consequences.

In November 2015, for example, Seraj al-Naeem, the founder of the online news outlet Awtar al-Aseel, was arrested and charged with libel under the IT Crime Act for sending a WhatsApp message that accused a doctor of medical malpractice. Al-Naeem was detained for hours and released on bail, but not before he was asked to surrender his smartphone to the police as evidence. Al-Naeem was subsequently charged for inquiring about the legality of surrendering his phone. He was acquitted of all charges in May.

In November an activist was broadcasting live on Facebook, showing empty streets in downtown Khartoum as evidence of a successful civil disobedience campaign when security services confronted and detained him for several days.

In January the administrator of a WhatsApp group for journalists was charged with libel under the IT Crime Act for a message that criticized the minister of health. He was detained and questioned for several hours along with the individual who sent the original message; both were subsequently released on bail and as of October still awaiting trial.

Cybercafes lacked privacy and were subject to intrusive government surveillance. In February, NISS and Ministry of Interior special cybercrime units raided 130 internet cafes in Khartoum in search of content threatening "public morals."

Academic Freedom and Cultural Events

The government restricted academic freedom at cultural and academic institutions. It determined the curriculums and appointed the vice chancellors responsible for administration. It continued to arrest student activists and cancel or deny permits for some student events. Youth activists reported some universities discouraged students from participating in antigovernment rallies and showed favorable treatment towards NCP students. Some professors exercised self-censorship. Security forces used tear gas and other heavy-handed tactics against largely peaceful protests at universities or involving university students. The Public Order Police continued to monitor public gatherings and cultural events, often intimidating women and girls, who feared police would arrest them for "indecent" dress or actions.

Following widespread unrest on college campuses across the country in April, many universities indefinitely suspended student activities (political, cultural, and social) on university premises and required approval before events could be held.

On April 30, NISS prevented the Sudanese Journalists' Network from holding a conference in Khartoum and provided no explanation. On September 13, NISS prevented the Sudanese Congress Party from holding a public event commemorating the third anniversary of the September 2013 protests, during which 185 to 200 protesters were killed.

b. Freedom of Peaceful Assembly and Association

Freedom of Assembly

Although the Interim National Constitution and law provide for freedom of assembly, the government severely restricted this right. The criminal code considers gatherings of more than five persons without a permit to be illegal. Organizers must notify the government 36 hours prior to assemblies and rallies.

In February, NISS dispersed a peaceful protest against the construction of new dams in Northern State, arrested a number of protesters, and later released them.

In April NISS arrested 27 students, including five female students, who were involved in protests at the University of Khartoum. The students protested April 11 to 14, following reports the government planned to sell the main campus to foreign investors. NISS released the 27 students without charge on April 16. An additional University of Khartoum student arrested separately but in conjunction with the protests, Asim Omer, remained detained and was charged after three months with the murder of a police officer, a capital offense, during campus protests. Human rights observers and classmates of Omer insisted the charges were based on falsified evidence, asserting the student was not present during the campus protests. As of year's end, trials of the students continued.

On November 20, NISS arrested without charge 28 college students who demonstrated on Africa Road against the government's austerity measures (fuel subsidy cuts) and subsequent price increases. The judge released all 28 students on bail November 21, and the students faced trials on November 22 and 23. On December 4, cases of all 28 students were dismissed. The arrests of the students were concurrent with a large-scale NISS arrest campaign, during which NISS detained 22 leading figures from the Sudan Congress Party (see section 1.e.) and several members of the National Unionist Party (NUP), Sudanese Communist Party, Arab Ba'ath Party, National Consensus Forces, and the Reform Now Movement, as well as civil society activists and journalists.

The government continued to deny permission to Islamic orders associated with opposition political parties, particularly the Ansar (Umma Party) and Khatmiya (Democratic Unionist Party), to hold large gatherings in public spaces, but parties regularly held opposition rallies on private property. Government security agents occasionally attended opposition meetings, disrupted opposition rallies, or summoned participants to security headquarters for questioning after meetings.

Authorities reportedly took only limited, if any, action against security force members who used excessive force. In November 2015 media reported the Ministry of Justice agreed to pay *diya* (blood money) totaling 35 million SDG ($5.3 million) in compensation to families of identified victims of the September

2013 protests and lift the immunity of four security officers. As of year's end, cases against the security officers remained pending (see section 1.a.).

Freedom of Association

The Interim National Constitution and law provide for freedom of association, but the government severely restricted this right. The law prohibits political parties linked to armed opposition groups. The government closed civil society organizations or refused to register them on several occasions. Government and security forces continued arbitrarily to enforce provisions of the NGO law, including measures that strictly regulate an organization's ability to receive foreign financing and register public activities.

Throughout the year, according to the Sudanese Confederation of Civil Society, authorities either rejected or failed to approve applications to reregister more than 40 registered organizations and began investigations into their activities.

Under the government's "Sudanization" policy, many organizations reported they faced administrative difficulties if they refused to have progovernment groups implement their programs at the state level. In Blue Nile, for example, HAC authorities prevented one humanitarian organization from implementing a food security program for several months until it agreed to collaborate with CORD, a local organization selected by the state government.

Organizations reported delays in obtaining permits to hold general assembly meetings. In the absence of general assemblies, the government prevented some organizations from holding elections or filling vacant positions. Some civil society activists believed the government delayed these approvals to disrupt the organizations' work or force them out of compliance with government regulations.

On February 29, NISS officers raided the Khartoum Center for Training and Human Development (TRACKS), a civil society capacity-building organization, for the second time in less than a year. The officers confiscated five laptops and nine telephones belonging to staff, trainees, and visitors. They collected documents, publications, flip charts, passports, and car keys belonging to the TRACKS directors, Khalaf-Allah al-Afif Muktar and Midhat Afifaddin Hamadan. Before departing the officers returned the equipment belonging to trainees and allowed them to leave. They also instructed Midhat, as well as Abuhrira Abdelrahman, another TRACKS staff member, and Adam Finun, an artist who happened to be visiting TRACKS at the time, to report to NISS headquarters in central Khartoum on March 3 before they were later released. In March NISS agents detained Director Khalafalla, Office Supervisor al-Shazali Ibrahim al-Sheikh, and Mustafa Adam, director of sister organization al-Zarqaa who was visiting TRACKS, and interrogated them separately before releasing them in intervals. One detainee who suffered from diabetes was deprived of food during his daylong detention.

Between March 3 and 13, NISS summoned and interrogated multiple activists associated with TRACKS, questioning all about their activities and relationship with the al-Khatim Adlan Center for Enlightenment and Human Development, an organization forcibly shut down by the government in 2012. Multiple activists were arrested and released in association with TRACKS through May.

On May 21, NISS arrested Khalaf-Allah al-Afif Muktar, Mustafa Adam and Midhat Afifaddin Hamadan from their homes and held them in cells with reported dimensions of 13 feet by 13 feet, which held over 26 prisoners, and had no ventilation. Due to the harsh conditions, Khalafalla, who had a heart condition, fainted on August 14 after being refused medical care three weeks previously. On August 15, the three detainees were transferred to al-Huda Prison in Omdurman North to face capital charges, including Article 50 (Undermining the Constitutional System), Article 51 (Waging War against the State), Article 53 (Espionage), and Article 65 (Criminal and Terrorist Organizations). In addition to these charges, Mustafa Adam and Midhat Afifaddin Hamadan faced charges related to the Information Crimes Law.

Three additional TRACKS associates, Arwa al-Rabie, Imany-Leila Ray, and al-Hassan Kheiry, who were arrested and released on bail after 10 days of detention in May, faced the same four charges as above. As of year's end, trials continued for all six individuals related to the TRACKS raid on February 29, three of whom were still in custody.

On May 5, a group of armed NISS officers raided the offices of prominent human rights lawyer Nabil Adeeb in Khartoum. At the time of the raid, Nabil Adeeb, chairperson of the Khartoum-based Sudanese Human Rights Monitor, was meeting with a group of students, some of whom had recently been dismissed or suspended from the University of Khartoum following the April protests. NISS arrested 10 students at the office, together with two lawyers and two female employees.

During the armed raid, NISS officers seized legal files and equipment, including

Adeeb's personal laptop, without a warrant. With the exception of Adeeb's cell phone, none of his property was returned.

Two National Umma Party (NUP) members, brothers Emad and Erwa al-Siddiq, were arrested and detained by NISS on December 14, 2015 and January 6 respectively. NISS charged the brothers with capital crimes and other charges, including undermining the constitution, warring against the state, affiliation with terrorist organizations, defamation, and criminal plotting. The charges were prompted by the brothers posting statements online critical of NISS, to include GPS coordinates of reported "ghost-houses" where NISS agents reportedly detained and physically abused human rights activists. Observers believed NISS sought to make an example of the case to discourage subversive political activities from both the Umma Party and the broader opposition. Emad al-Siddiq was convicted on September 5 and sentenced to six months' imprisonment, which he had already served. As such, he was released the day of the ruling and fined 10,000 SDG ($1,500). Erwa al-Siddiq was also convicted and sentenced to one year in prison; he was released in September. Erwa was also fined 20,000 SDG ($3,000).

In November and December, authorities arrested the entire senior leadership of the Sudan Congress Party, and detained them without charges and, with one exception, without visitation. NISS released the opposition members in late December with no charges.

c. Freedom of Religion

See the Department of State's *International Religious Freedom Report* at www.state.gov/religiousfreedomreport/.

d. Freedom of Movement, Internally Displaced Persons, Protection of Refugees, and Stateless Persons

The Interim National Constitution and law provide for freedom of movement, foreign travel, emigration, and repatriation, but the government restricted these rights for foreigners, including humanitarian workers.

The government impeded the work of UN agencies and delayed full approval of their activities throughout the country, particularly in the Two Areas. NGOs also alleged the government impeded humanitarian assistance in the Two Areas.

<u>Abuse of Migrants, Refugees, and Stateless Persons</u>: Asylum seekers and refugees were vulnerable to arbitrary arrest and harassment outside of camps because they did not receive identification cards while awaiting government determination of refugee or asylum status. Refugees and asylum seekers in urban areas were also subject to arrest because the government's encampment policy makes it illegal to move from assigned camps without authorization. On average 150-200 refugees and asylum seekers were detained in Khartoum each month and assisted with legal aid by the joint UNHCR and commissioner for refugees legal team. Although the Asylum Act makes naturalization possible for refugees, it was not fully implemented.

There were some reported abuses, including gender-based violence, in the camps. The government worked closely with UNHCR to provide greater protection to refugees. There were government impediments relating to access to refugees, including delay or denial of travel permits and visa approvals.

According to human rights advocates, the delay in granting legal status was partly the reason some new refugees left the camps before registering with UNHCR. Refugees often relied on human trafficking and smuggling networks to leave camps. Traffickers routinely abused and tortured refugees if ransoms were not paid.

See the Department of State's *Trafficking in Persons Report* at www.state.gov/j/tip/rls/tiprpt/.

<u>In-country Movement</u>: The government and rebels restricted the movement of citizens as well as UN and humanitarian organization personnel in conflict areas (see section 1.g.). While the government claimed refugees had freedom of movement within the country, it required they formally register and be granted travel permits before leaving refugee camps. According to authorities, registration of refugees helped provide their personal security. Refugees faced administrative fines once they returned to their camp, if they left camps without permission and were intercepted by authorities.

Internal movement was generally unhindered for citizens outside conflict areas. Foreigners needed travel permits for domestic travel outside Khartoum, which were often difficult to obtain. Foreigners were required to register with the Ministry of Interior's Alien Control Division within three days of arrival and were limited to a 15.5-mile radius from Khartoum. Once registered, foreigners were allowed to move beyond this radius, but travel outside of Khartoum State required official approval.

The government delayed issuing humanitarian visas to UN and NGO staff and generally denied access to conflict areas, with some exceptions made for Darfur IDP camps. The government also delayed issuing travel permits to nonconflict areas.

The country maintained a reservation on Article 26 of the UN Convention on Refugees of 1951 regarding refugees' right to move freely and choose their place of residence within a country. The government's encampment policy requires asylum seekers and refugees to stay in designated camps. The government allowed for the establishment of two camps for South Sudanese refugees in East Darfur. The government increasingly referred to "holding sites" in White Nile as refugee camps.

Foreign Travel: The government requires citizens to obtain an exit visa if they wish to depart the country. Issuance was usually without complication, but the government continued to use the visa requirement to restrict some citizens' travel, especially persons of political or security interest. To obtain an exit visa, children must receive the permission of both parents.

In March, five civil society representatives (Faisal Mohamed Salih, Siddig Yousif, Muawia Shaddad, Sawasan Alshoaya, and Salih Mahmoud) were stopped by plainclothes security officials at Khartoum International Airport traveling to Geneva, where they were to participate in UN presession meetings of the universal periodic review (UPR) for Sudan. Their passports were confiscated, and they were told to report to NISS headquarters for further information to reclaim them, thereby preventing them from attending the Geneva meetings.

On November 19, NISS agents again prevented Siddig Yousif of the Solidarity Committee from traveling to Geneva to participate in civil society/political meetings. According to Yousif, this incident was the fifth time within two years that NISS imposed a travel ban on him.

Exile: The government observed the law prohibiting forced exile. It warned political opponents of their potential arrest, however, if they returned. Opposition leaders and NGO activists remained in self-imposed exile in northern Africa and Europe; other activists fled the country during the year. In September 2015 a presidential decree granted general amnesty for opposition members and rebel leaders living abroad who agreed to return to Sudan to participate in the national dialogue. As of year's end, prominent opposition members had not returned to the country under the amnesty, some expressing concern about their civic and political rights even with the amnesty (see section 1.d.).

Internally Displaced Persons

Large-scale displacement continued to be a severe problem in Darfur and the Two Areas, and government restrictions and security constraints continued to limit access to affected populations and impeded the delivery of humanitarian services.

According to the United Nations and partners, during the first 11 months of the year, an estimated 97,500 persons were reported newly displaced across Darfur. Up to an additional 88,775 persons were also reported displaced, but the United Nations reported its inability to verify these figures due to lack of access to the relevant locations. In addition, approximately 38,150 persons reportedly returned, of which 25,564 (in Golo) were verified by the WFP. UN OCHA reported the vast majority of the displacement during the year was triggered by the conflict in the Jebel Marra area, which ignited in January. The United Nations and partners reported during the year through December, 3,026 individuals were newly displaced in Southern and Western Kordofan and Blue Nile, although the number was largely unknown due to lack of access to those areas. Other reports placed the number of displaced at 12,468. Many IDPs faced chronic food shortages and inadequate medical care. Significant numbers of farmers were prevented from planting their fields due to the conflict, leading to near-famine conditions in parts of Southern Kordofan. The government and the SPLM-N continued to deny access to humanitarian actors and UN agencies in areas controlled by the SPLM-N; these areas contained approximately 800,000 of the IDPs and severely affected persons in 2015. UN agencies could provide no estimates citing lack of access as a hindrance.

Government restrictions, harassment, and the threat of expulsion resulted in continued interruption of gender-based violence programming. Reporting and outreach were limited (see section 5). Some UN agencies were able to work with the Darfur governor's advisers on women and children to raise awareness of gender-based violence and response efforts.

There were numerous reports of abuse committed by government security forces, rebels, and armed groups against IDPs in Darfur, including rapes and beatings (see section 1.g.).

Outside IDP camps and towns, insecurity restricted freedom of movement, and women and girls who left the towns and camps risked sexual violence. Insecurity within IDP camps also was a problem. The government provided little assistance or protection to IDPs in Darfur. Most IDP camps had no functioning police force. International observers noted criminal gangs aligned with rebel groups operated openly in several IDP camps.

As in previous years, the government did not establish formal IDP or refugee camps in Khartoum or the Two Areas, and UNHCR did not make any formal requests to establish such new camps during the year.

The United Nations did not have a presence in SPLM-N-controlled areas and was unable to assess the scope of civilian displacement in the area.

Protection of Refugees

As of November UNHCR reported approximately 403,000 refugees and asylum seekers in the country, including 106,000 Eritreans, 15,000 Ethiopians, and 8,000 Chadians. Unlike in previous years, Chadian population numbers considered only those in camps, and not those spontaneously settled along the border and among the population. As of November more than 262,000 South Sudanese had arrived in the country since fighting erupted in December 2013, including a new influx in East Darfur.

New Eritrean refugees entering eastern Sudan often stayed in camps for two to three months before moving to Khartoum, other parts of the country, or on to Libya in an effort to reach Europe. The government continued to restrict access in eastern Sudan for international humanitarian NGOs, as it did throughout the country.

According to UNHCR, the government hosted approximately 67,000 refugees in Khartoum as of October.

From January to June, an estimated 7,500 persons fled Southern Kordofan to become refugees in South Sudan, nearly 3,000 of whom arrived in May alone. Nearly 90 percent were women and children, with one child in 10 arriving alone or without a family member.

As of November UNHCR estimated 350,000 persons of South Sudanese origin remained in the country following South Sudan's independence in 2011. Approximately 250,000 of them lived in Khartoum, many integrated into the urban population. An estimated 40,000 lived in shantytowns, informal settlements known as "open areas" until August. The government did not officially recognize this population as refugees or IDPs and restricted access to these areas by humanitarian organizations. Many open areas lacked basic services such as water, electricity, and sewage systems. In August authorities relocated more than 6,000 South Sudanese from three open areas in Ombeda locality to a new site in Nivasha. UNHCR, which was not informed in advance about the relocation, expressed concern over how the relocation was carried out. Access to basic services in the new site remained limited.

UNHCR reported 40,000 persons of South Sudanese origin who had remained in the country following South Sudan's independence had obtained nationality documents from the South Sudan Consulate in Khartoum as of December. The governments of Sudan and South Sudan signed a framework agreement (known as the "four freedoms" agreement) as part of a broader bilateral agreement in 2012 which provides for citizens of both states to enjoy freedom of residence, movement, economic activity, and property ownership, but it was not fully implemented during the year.

The government did not recognize individuals fleeing from South Sudan as refugees under the 1951 Refugee Convention but essentially treated them as such under the Arab/Islamic regime of asylum following December 2013 fighting in South Sudan, and it allowed some national and international organizations to assist them. In 2014 UNHCR and the Ministry of Interior's Commission for Refugees and Directorate General of Passports and Immigration signed a memorandum of understanding (MOU) on the registration and documentation of approximately 500,000 South Sudanese in Sudan, including those that fled the conflict in South Sudan in December 2013.

On March 17, the government directed that South Sudanese were to be treated as foreigners. In April UNHCR reported on the arrests of 189 South Sudanese refugees mostly around the Alsog al-Markazee area in Khartoum for alleged lack of documentation or nonrecognition of the documents issued by the Department of Passports and Immigration Police. The individuals incurred fines of approximately 1,112 SDG ($167). The government released approximately 300 South Sudanese following intervention by UNHCR, but many remained in detention, per UNHCR reports. UNHCR successfully challenged convictions based on nonrecognition of the Immigration Police-issued documents before the Fourth Circuit of the Supreme Court.

On September 1, UNHCR and the Office of the Commission for Refugees signed a MOU designed to regulate how the two entities would manage South Sudanese refugees. UNHCR noted that although the government desired to distinguish among South Sudanese refugees based on refugees' date of arrival in the country, the agreement itself contains no such distinctions. In December the government allegedly confirmed the content of the MOU, lifting the previous position of a cut-off date based on arrival in the country.

<u>Access to Asylum</u>: The government generally provided first asylum/temporary protection to individuals who might not qualify as refugees. In 2014 the government adopted asylum legislation that provides for the granting of asylum or refugee status and requires asylum applications to be nominally submitted within 30 days of arrival in the country. This time stipulation was not strictly enforced. The government granted asylum to many asylum seekers, particularly from Eritrea, Syria, Somalia, and Ethiopia, but it sometimes considered individuals registered as asylum seekers or refugees in another country, mostly in Ethiopia, to be irregular movers or migrants. Government officials routinely took up to three months to approve individual refugee and asylum status, but they worked with UNHCR to implement status determination procedures in eastern Sudan and Darfur and attempted to reduce the case backlog. The law requires asylum seekers to register both as refugees with the Commission for Refugees and as foreigners with the Civil Registry (to obtain a "foreign" number).

In August security officials told reporters that 816 African migrants (and Sudanese intending to emigrate) and a group of smugglers were arrested near the country's border with Libya between June and August. The officials said the migrants were attempting to cross into Libya with plans to proceed to Europe. Among those arrested were 347 Eritreans, 130 Ethiopians, and 90 Sudanese; the remainder were mostly Somalis. Foreign individuals were charged, convicted, and deported to their countries of origin. The status of the Sudanese who were apprehended was unknown. Since the beginning of the Syrian conflict in 2011, more than 40,000 Syrians have arrived in Sudan, according to government sources, of whom 6,990 have been registered with UNHCR. The government did not require visas or residency permits for Syrians out of Arab solidarity. The Sudanese Commission for Refugees, however, restarted registration of Syrian nationals in November 2015 to better account for their number and needs.

The government waives regular entry visa requirements for Yemenis. As of November, more than 1,600 Yemeni refugees had registered in Sudan.

Refoulement: The country is a signatory to the 1951 Convention relating to the Status of Refugees and generally respected the international principle of nonrefoulement with a few notable exceptions. According to UNHCR incidents of refoulement decreased significantly during the year. In early May authorities arrested 377 individuals in Dongola, Northern State, as they attempted to cross the country's northwest border into Libya. The group included 313 Eritreans and 64 Ethiopians. Six were already registered refugees within Sudan. All faced charges of illegal entry and were tried in court. On May 22, the authorities deported all Ethiopian refugees and Eritrean refugees, which included 14 children.

In February 2015 authorities in the east disclosed they followed a practice of returning "recyclers"--Eritrean asylum seekers presumed to be previously registered as refugees in Ethiopia.

With UNHCR's intervention, authorities were trained on referral procedures to prevent refoulement, including of refugees who previously registered in other countries.

Employment: The government in principle allows refugees to work informally but rarely granted work permits (even to refugees who have obtained higher degrees in the country). In 2015 and during the year, UNHCR signed a project partnership agreement with the Commission for Refugees to issue over 1,000 work permits to selected refugees for a livelihood graduation program implemented in Kassala and Gadaref. In 2015 some refugee beneficiaries were selected, but the issuance of permits was still pending at year's end.

Some refugees in eastern states were able to find informal work as agricultural workers or laborers in towns. Many women in camps reportedly resorted to illegal production of alcohol and were subjected to arrest and harassment by police. In urban centers the majority of refugees worked in the informal sector (for example, as tea sellers, house cleaners, and drivers), leaving them at heightened risk of arrest, exploitation, and abuse.

Temporary Protection: The government generally maintained an open border with South Sudan. The government position on the status of South Sudanese in Sudan, however, changed on multiple occasions based on improvements or contentious points in the Sudan-South Sudan relationship. Before signing a September MOU with UNHCR, which officially recognized South Sudanese in Sudan as refugees, there were statements by the government both that South Sudanese refugees fleeing conflict in their country would enjoy the same status as Sudanese citizens, and that they would be treated as foreigners when relations encountered setbacks. As of November, UNHCR estimated 263,425 individuals had crossed into the country from South Sudan since December 2013, with more than 110,000 refugees having arrived since January. The majority sought refuge in White Nile State.

Since December 2013 more than approximately 35,000 South Sudanese also traveled to Khartoum.

Stateless Persons

The 1994 Nationality Act was amended in 2005 not only to apply to child with a father of Sudanese decent but also to allow a child born to a Sudanese mother to acquire Sudanese nationality by birth by following an application process. The Interim Sudanese Constitution, however, provides "every person born to a Sudanese mother or father shall have an inalienable right to enjoy Sudanese nationality and citizenship." After the creation of the independent State of South Sudan, the Republic of Sudan amended its nationality law in 2011 but has yet to amend the relevant sections of the 1994 Act. The Interim Sudanese Constitution remains in force until Sudan adopts a permanent constitution.

Persons of South Sudanese origin who lived for many years in the Republic of Sudan were stripped of their Sudanese nationality by law, irrespective of the strength of their connections to the new state of South Sudan or Sudan and their views on which state to which they wished to belong. Other populations who risked being adversely affected included individuals with one parent from Sudan and one from South Sudan; members of cross-border ethnic groups; and persons separated from their families by war, including unaccompanied children.

Some persons of South Sudanese origin living in Sudan risked ending up stateless, without either a Sudanese or South Sudanese nationality, and losing their basic rights.

Section 3. Freedom to Participate in the Political Process

The country continued to operate under the Interim National Constitution of the Comprehensive Peace Agreement (CPA). The constitution provides citizens the ability to choose their government in free and fair periodic elections based on universal and equal suffrage. Citizens were unable to exercise this right in practice. Post-CPA provisions provide for a referendum on the status of Abyei and popular consultations in Blue Nile and Southern Kordofan. In Abyei the Ngok Dinka held a unilateral referendum in October 2013, which the international community did not recognize. No popular consultations took place during the year in either Southern Kordofan or Blue Nile.

Several parts of the CPA, designed to clarify the status of southern-aligned groups remaining in the north following South Sudan's secession continued to be the subject of negotiations between the governments of Sudan, South Sudan, and rebel groups. Peace negotiations for the Two Areas and Darfur continued to stall while fighting between government and antigovernment forces continued. Neither Sudan nor South Sudan progressed toward a resolution on the final status of Abyei.

The Darfur Referendum, which took place April 11-13, was conducted to determine whether Darfur would be administered via the current system of five states or as one regional administration. Observers from the African Union and the League of Arab States monitored the referendum. The Darfur Referendum Commission announced on April 14 that 97.27 percent of voters had opted to keep Darfur's current administrative configuration. Human rights observers said the government believed a unified Darfur would give rebels a platform to push for independence just as South Sudan did successfully in 2011.

Elections and Political Participation

<u>Recent Elections</u>: The national-level executive and legislative elections, held April 13-16, 2015, did not meet international standards. The government failed to create a free, fair, and conducive elections environment. Restrictions on political rights and freedoms, lack of a credible national dialogue, and the continuation of armed conflict on the country's peripheries contributed to a very low voter turnout. Observers noted numerous problems with the preelection environment. The legal framework did not protect basic freedoms of assembly, speech, and press. Security forces restricted the actions of opposition parties and arrested opposition members and supporters. Additionally, there were reported acts of violence during the election period (see section 1.c.).

The main opposition parties, Umma National Party, National Consensus Forces, Sudanese Congress Party, Sudanese Communist Party, and the Popular Congress Party, boycotted the election; only the ruling NCP party and National Unity parties participated.

According to the chair of the National Election Commission, 5,584,863 votes were counted in the election, representing approximately a 46 percent participation rate. According to the AU and other observers, however, turnout was considerably lower. Following the elections the National Assembly consisted of 426 seats (Upper House). The NCP held 323 seats, Democratic Unionist Party 25, and independents 19 seats; other minor political parties won the remaining seats. The independents, many of whom were previously ejected from the ruling NCP, were prevented by the government from forming a parliamentary group. The States Council (Lower House) consisted of 54 members with each state represented by three members. The NCP had 36 members in the Lower House.

General elections for president and the National Assembly are scheduled to be held every five years. The next general election is scheduled for 2020. The previous (nation-wide excluding conflict areas) gubernatorial election was held in April 2010. The National Assembly changed the constitution in January 2015 to authorize the president to appoint the governors instead of the voter selecting them. Under this amendment, Bashir appointed 18 state governors.

Political Parties and Political Participation: The NCP dominated the political landscape, controlling all of the regional governorships and holding a two-thirds majority in the National Assembly. Other parties held the remaining seats, with the Original Democratic Unionist Party holding 25 seats, independents holding 19, and the Registered Faction Democratic Unionist Party holding 15 seats.

The Political Parties Affairs Council listed 92 registered political parties; organizers of the national dialogue concurred there were more than 90 political parties. The Umma Party and the Democratic Unionist Party were never registered with the government. The Reform Now Party registered as a political party during the year. A new political coalition, the Future Forces for Change, was established and included the Reform Now Party, Justice Forum for Peace, and disaffected former NCP member Farah Aggar. The government continued to harass some opposition leaders who spoke with representatives of foreign organizations or embassies or travelled abroad (see section 2.d.).

The Political Parties Affairs Council oversees the registration of political parties. The ruling party controls the council; it is not an independent body. The council continued to refuse to register the Republican (Jamhori) Party, which opposes Islamic extremism and promotes secularism. The party leader condemned the decision and filed a complaint in the Constitutional Court.

Authorities monitored and impeded political party meetings and activities, restricted political party demonstrations, used excessive force to break them up, and arrested opposition party members.

In January 2014 the president announced a national dialogue to engage all political parties, including the opposition, civil society, and others, in a planning framework to recommend, initiate, and implement democratic reforms. The government also described the dialogue as a mechanism for resolving conflicts throughout the country and determining a constitutional framework. While some opposition groups agreed to participate, most major opposition parties withdrew from the dialogue early in 2014.

Early in 2015 the government announced it would postpone holding a national dialogue until after national elections in April 2015, and it amended the Interim National Constitution. In March 2015 the government failed to attend an AU-facilitated meeting aimed at securing inclusion of opposition and armed groups in the national dialogue. Nonetheless, in August 2015 President Bashir chaired a meeting of the High Coordinating Committee of the National Dialogue. The government launched the dialogue in October 2015, although major opposition parties and rebel groups continued to boycott the process.

On October 10, the government concluded its two-year-long national dialogue process, bringing in regional officials, such as the Egyptian and Ugandan presidents, to support claims the process was legitimate and inclusive. President Bashir announced a two-month extension of the ceasefire in Darfur and the Two Areas of South Kordofan and Blue Nile to convey sincerity in establishing a new political path forward. In a move that observers regarded as an outgrowth of the national dialogue, in late December, parliament voted to reinstate the post of prime minister, a position that was abolished in 1989, after Bashir came to power.

<u>Participation of Women and Minorities</u>: Women have the right to vote. In July 2014 the National Assembly increased from 25 to 30 percent the proportion of seats in the national and state assemblies drawn from state-level women's lists.

A few religious minorities participated in government. There were prominent Coptic Christian politicians within the National Assembly, Khartoum city government, and Khartoum state assembly. A member of the national election commission was Coptic. A female Anglican served as the state minister of water resources and electricity.

Section 4. Corruption and Lack of Transparency in Government

The law provides criminal penalties for corruption by officials; nevertheless, government corruption at all levels was widespread. The government made few efforts to enforce legislation aimed at preventing and prosecuting corruption.

Corruption: According to the World Bank's most recent Worldwide Governance Indicators, corruption was a severe problem. The law provides the legislative framework for addressing official corruption, but implementation was weak, and many punishments were lenient. Officials found guilty of corrupt acts could often avoid jail time if they returned ill-gotten funds. Journalists who reported on government corruption were sometimes intimidated, detained, and interrogated by services.

A special anticorruption attorney investigates and tries corruption cases involving officials, their spouses, and their children. Punishments for embezzlement include imprisonment or execution for public service workers, although these sanctions were almost never carried out. All bank employees are considered public service workers.

In August 2015 the Council of Ministers chaired by the minister of the presidency endorsed the National Anti-corruption Commission Bill for 2015, presented by the minister of justice. The bill aimed to establish an anticorruption commission for all levels of government to boost transparency in financial and administrative transactions. As of July the president had returned the bill to the National Assembly where it remained pending review in December.

Reporting on corruption was considered a "red line" set by NISS and a topic authorities for the most part prohibited newspapers from covering (section 2.a.).

Financial Disclosure: The law requires high officials to disclose publicly income and assets. There are no clear sanctions for noncompliance, although the commission possesses discretionary powers to punish violators. The Financial Disclosure and Inspection Committee and the Unlawful and Suspicious Enrichment Administration at the Justice Ministry both monitored compliance. Despite two different bodies ostensibly charged with combating official corruption, there was no effective enforcement or prosecution of offenders.

<u>Public Access to Information</u>: In January 2015 the government passed a freedom of information law to promote greater transparency and allow citizens greater access to information. As of August local and international human rights observers and journalists remained skeptical the law would improve access to information given that little information was publicly disseminated about the law. The law exempts 12 categories of information that can be maintained as classified, including personal information and information on national security, foreign policy, and criminal procedures.

Section 5. Governmental Attitude Regarding International and Nongovernmental Investigation of Alleged Violations of Human Rights

The government was uncooperative with, and unresponsive to, domestic human rights groups. It restricted and harassed workers of both domestic and international human rights organizations (See section 1.g. for government denial of requests to investigate Amnesty International allegations).

According to international NGOs, government agents consistently monitored, threatened, prosecuted, and occasionally physically assaulted civil society activists. The government arrested NGO-affiliated international human rights and humanitarian workers, including in Darfur (see section 1.g.).

NGOs must register with the HAC, the government entity for regulating humanitarian efforts. The HAC obstructed the work of NGOs including in Darfur, the Two Areas, White Nile State, and Abyei. The HAC often changed its rules and regulations without prior notification.

Throughout the year, the HAC continued to require NGOs to refrain from interviewing or selecting staff unless they used a five-person government selection panel with HAC officials present. This requirement significantly delayed the hiring of new staff in Darfur. The HAC also continued to impose additional requirements on humanitarian organizations, often at the state level. In late December the HAC issued new guidelines to ease restrictions on movement of humanitarian workers; however, the guidelines were not implemented by year's end.

UN agencies experienced constraints regarding access, although the government granted some travel permits to Central, South, and West Darfur. UNAMID was sometimes denied access to provide security to UN and other humanitarian actors. In these cases the humanitarian agencies had to rely on government-provided security escorts. The government, however, frequently declined to provide them escorts to areas affected by fighting and restricted movement of UN-sponsored fuel, food, and nonfood supplies to areas outside of major population centers. UNAMID continued to experience flight restrictions. UNAMID flights were also regularly cancelled due to the lack of clearance by the authorities. These included repeated cancellations of flights to Sortony, North Darfur. On April 15, UNAMID aircraft flying to Misteri, West Darfur, had to modify their usual flight route following threats from the government that it would shoot down UN flights over the Sudanese-Chadian joint forces camps.

Darfur reportedly hosted some 3.3 million persons in need of humanitarian assistance, of whom 1.6 million were in camps, according to OCHA. Nonetheless, the government continued to push for a reduced role of the international humanitarian community in the country. Restrictions on entry visas and renewal of residency permits were frequently used to limit humanitarian action and, in some cases, as a means of expelling humanitarian personnel. Additionally, restrictions on movements and denial of access and clearances continued to be imposed on humanitarian agencies by the authorities. The result has been a steady reduction in humanitarian operational capacity in Darfur and other areas of the country.

Rebel-held areas in Jebel Marra remained cut off from humanitarian access. There were numerous examples similar to the following: While an emergency food distribution was carried out by the WFP in Fanga Suk, Nertiti, and Thur, lack of access and administrative restrictions prevented food distribution in Guldo, Rockero, and Golo, and delayed nonfood item distribution in Guldo and Thur.

According to UNAMID the government forbade numerous land movements and planned flights for UNAMID and humanitarian organizations to access sites in Darfur, mostly in North and Central Darfur. Access limitations and fear of government retribution continued to inhibit reporting on human rights violations, especially sexual and gender-based abuses.

The government granted the UNAMID Human Rights Section one visa in November, and the vacancy rate remained at 57 per cent. The visa request for the chief of the Protection of Civilians Section remained outstanding. In the 2016/17 budget, the General Assembly abolished 10 posts that had remained vacant for more than three years owing to visa denials, which included those of senior women protection adviser and the senior planning officer.

In December 2015 NISS closed seven offices of Tearfund, an international NGO that was providing health and nutrition services in Central Darfur. No reason was given for the closure or its anticipated duration. On January 12, the government canceled Tearfund's registration. Human rights advocates and humanitarian aid workers viewed the actions as more restrictions on the humanitarian operating environment.

The government continued to use bureaucratic impediments to restrict the actions of humanitarian organizations, contrary to provisions in the 2007 joint communique between the government and the United Nations. These included delaying the issuance of visas and travel permits to humanitarian workers and limiting their validity to less than six months. In some instances authorities only renewed visas for 10-day periods, greatly affecting UNAMID's ability to carry out its operations. Authorities also delayed the release of food and necessary equipment to UNAMID for prolonged periods. Members of the UN Security Council expressed grave concern about the bureaucratic and operational restrictions faced by UNAMID, including the government's regular holding of UNAMID containers containing food rations for peacekeepers and its continued delay of visa approvals for UNAMID personnel. The government allowed no humanitarian access to Jebel Marra (see section 1.g.).

Humanitarian organizations reported the government continued to deny travel to East Darfur and severely limited travel to South Darfur. Some travel to Central, North, and West Darfur, as well as eastern Sudan and White Nile state, was approved.

<u>The United Nations or Other International Bodies</u>: The government remained uncooperative with UN Security Council Resolution 1593 and failed to comply with the ICC arrest warrants for President Bashir; Ahmad Muhammad Haroun, former minister for humanitarian affairs and current governor of Northern Kordofan; former defense minister and current governor of Khartoum State, Abd al-Rahim Hussein; Abdallah Banda Abakaer Nourain, a militia leader who fought against the government; and Ali Muhammad Abd al-Rahman Hussein, a senior Jingaweit commander, who supported the government against Darfur rebel groups.

In 2005 the United Nations established a sanctions regime on Sudan pursuant to Resolution 1591. These sanctions impose an arms embargo on Darfur and travel bans and asset freezes of certain individuals. A panel of experts, appointed by the UN Sanctions Committee, prepared quarterly reports regarding compliance with Resolution 1591, which informs an annual Sanctions Committee report. In its

January and October reports, the panel of experts indicated the country was not fully compliant with the Darfur sanctions regime.

The government is a party to the African Charter on Human and Peoples' Rights. The government last submitted a report to the African Commission in 2011. In 2014 the commission released its decision regarding a 2009 complaint filed against the government on behalf of IDPs regarding torture and other allegations. The commission ordered the country to pay compensation, initiate an investigation, amend legislation, and train security officers on the prohibition of torture. The government did not implement the commission's decision.

During the year the government generally cooperated with visits of the UN independent expert on the situation of human rights in Sudan, Aristide Nononsi. Nononsi was not generally granted meaningful access to the conflict areas of Sudan, and, while he met with some independent civil society organizations, most of his meetings were with government officials or government-aligned NGOs. Government officials tightly controlled his schedule, and his opportunities to meet with independent civil society organizations were few.

Section 6. Discrimination, Societal Abuses, and Trafficking in Persons

Women

The Ministry of Social Welfare, Women, and Child Affairs is responsible for matters pertaining to women. The Violence against Women Unit oversees branches in 14 of the 18 states and the National Action Plan for Combating Violence against Women. It monitors and reports on women-related issues and works with civil society and other stakeholders on issues of sexual and gender-based violence.

Rape and Domestic Violence: From January to December, UNAMID documented 100 cases involving 222 victims of conflict-related sexual violence compared with 80 cases and 105 victims in 2015. The victims included minors comprising 119 girls and one boy, whose ages ranged between eight and 17 years old. UNAMID received the cases from all five Darfur states. Underreporting remained prevalent, however, and UNAMID reported the figures were not representative of the reality on the ground.

There were no reliable statistics on the prevalence of such violence in other areas. The government rejected UNAMID figures on the basis that the cases had not been reported to state authorities, but observers concurred that the government needed capacity building in how to track cases. The international expert on the human rights situation in Sudan in his September report again cited a need for building government capacity for protection of women and children (see section 1.g.).

The UN special rapporteur on violence against women visited the country in May 2015 and determined violence against women and silence around the issue was of concern in both conflict and nonconflict areas. She urged the government "to set up a commission of inquiry, consisting of both national and international persons, to look into the reports of allegations of mass rapes in different regions, including recent allegations regarding the village of Thabit." As of year's end, no such investigation had taken place.

Female Genital Mutilation/Cutting (FGM/C): FGM/C traditionally was practiced in the country. The government launched a national campaign in 2008 to eradicate FGM/C by 2018. The government, with the support of the first lady, continued to prioritize the *saleema* (uncut) campaign, which raised public awareness about FGM/C throughout the year. The government agreed to a three-year program with the UN Children's Fund (UNICEF), UN Population Fund (UNFPA), and the World Health Organization (WHO) to seek to end FGM/C. As a result of the programming, 86 new communities declared keeping their girls saleema/uncut in North Kordofan, South Kordofan, South Darfur, Northern States, River Nile, and Blue Nile States, bringing the cumulative number of communities that have declared collective abandonment of FGM/C to 995 communities. On the household level, 10,437 parents committed to leave their daughters uncut in Khartoum and Northern States and Blue Nile.

FGM/C remained a problem for women and girls throughout the country. No national law prohibits FGM/C. Since 2008, however, five states have passed laws prohibiting FGM/C: South Kordofan, Gedaref, Red Sea, South Darfur, and West Darfur. In its October 2015 report, UNESCO expressed concern that the provisions criminalizing FGM/C were removed from the Child Health Act.

According to UNICEF and UNFPA, the national prevalence rate of FGM/C among girls and women between 15 and 49 years old was 86 percent, a 2 percent decrease from 2014. Prevalence varied geographically and depended on the local ethnic group. The 2010 Sudan Household Health Survey indicated prevalence rates of FGM/C varied from 99.4 per cent in Northern State to 68.4 per cent in Western Darfur.

Girls generally were cut when they were five to 11 years old. Comprehensive figures were not available. The government and UNICEF reported a shift in attitudes towards FGM/C and observed downward trends in its prevalence between the household health surveys in 2006 and 2010. The 2010 survey concluded 34.5 percent of girls between the ages five and nine years old were cut, compared with 41 percent in 2006. A 2015 survey showed 63.7 percent of circumcised women were cut between the ages of five and nine years old.

Of girls and women ages 15-19, 37 percent favored FGM/C in 2010, compared with 73 percent in 2006.

The government attempted to curb the prevalence of FGM/C and made public-awareness campaigns a top priority. In 2008 the National Council on Child Welfare, with support from UNICEF, launched the National Strategy to Abolish FGM/C in Sudan (2008-18).

In Geneva in March, the government accepted the Human Rights Council's UPR recommendations, including reforms on FGM/C and child marriage.

In October the Council of Ministers at the national level endorsed an amendment to the 1991 Criminal Act introducing a new article on FGM/C, which was under review in parliament. If passed, the new law would reportedly add a punishment of three years' imprisonment, along with fines and potential revocation of workplace licenses for offenders. The text had not been made available publicly.

Other Harmful Traditional Practices: The Interim National Constitution obligates states to combat harmful customs and traditions that undermine the dignity and status of women. Nonetheless, harmful traditional practices, such as early and forced marriages, continued (see section 6, Children).

Sexual Harassment: No law specifically prohibits sexual harassment, although the law prohibits gross indecency, which is defined as any act contrary to another person's modesty. Authorities generally enforced the statute. The penalty for gross indecency is imprisonment for up to one year and 40 lashes. There were frequent reports of sexual harassment by police. The government did not provide any access to information on the number of sexual harassment reports made. Most documentable efforts to curb sexual harassment were made by NGOs.

Reproductive Rights: Although awareness of reproductive rights was lacking in some communities, couples were generally able to decide the number, spacing, and timing of their children; manage their reproductive health; and have access to the means and information to do so, free from discrimination, coercion, or violence. Contraception, skilled medical attendance during childbirth, and obstetric and postpartum care were not always accessible in rural areas. The UN Development Program estimated that 13 percent of girls and women between the ages of 15 and 49 years old used a modern method of contraception in 2015. WHO estimated in 2013 that the maternal mortality rate was 360 deaths per 100,000 live births and that skilled healthcare personnel attended 31 percent of births. The high maternal mortality rate stemmed in large part from lack of access to reproductive health and emergency obstetric care, particularly in rural areas, lack of access to family planning services, poor sanitation, and chronic undernourishment in poorer areas, as well as infection, malaria, anemia, and hemorrhage.

Discrimination: The law, including many traditional legal practices and certain provisions of Islamic jurisprudence as interpreted and applied by the government, discriminates against women. In accordance with Islamic judicial interpretation, a Muslim widow inherits one-eighth of her husband's estate; of the remaining seven-eighths, two-thirds goes to the sons and one-third to the daughters. Depending on the wording of the marriage contract, it was often much easier for men than women to initiate legal divorce proceedings. In certain probate trials, the testimony of women is not considered equivalent to that of men; the testimony of two women is required. In other civil trials, the testimony of a woman equals that of a man.

A Muslim woman cannot legally marry a non-Muslim man. This prohibition usually was neither observed nor enforced among certain populations.

Various government institutions required women to dress according to Islamic or cultural standards, including wearing a head covering. In Khartoum, Public Order Police occasionally brought women before judges for allegedly violating Islamic standards. One women's advocacy group estimated that in Khartoum, Public Order Police arrested an average of 40 women per day.

Islamic standards for dress generally were not enforced for non-Muslims.

In addition to housing and education discrimination, women experienced economic discrimination in access to employment, equal pay for substantially similar work, credit, and owning or managing businesses.

Children

Birth Registration: The law grants citizenship to children born to a father who is a Sudanese national by descent. The Interim National Constitution states persons born to a Sudanese mother or father have the right to citizenship. Although the constitution eliminated gender discrimination in conferring nationality on children, the law does not grant gender equality in the passing of citizenship to children.

Most newborns had access to birth certificates, but some in remote areas did not. Registered midwives, dispensaries, clinics, and hospitals could issue certificates. A birth certificate does not automatically qualify a child for citizenship. Failure to present a valid birth certificate precludes enrollment in school. Access to health care was similarly dependent on possession of a valid birth certificate, but many doctors accepted a patient's verbal assurance that he or she had one.

Education: The law provides for tuition-free basic education up to grade eight, but students often had to pay school, uniform, and examination fees to attend. Primary education is neither compulsory nor universal. In Darfur few children outside of cities had access to primary education due to its high cost. In public schools boys and girls are educated separately in urban areas but often together in rural areas, where resources are more limited.

In 2013 the government reported that overall female enrollment increased to 69 percent, as the result of a national education strategy focused on girls.

A September 2015 Ministry of Education/UNICEF report estimated that 15 percent of primary school children were at risk of dropping out before the final grade of primary school; the report identified girls, IDPs, children in rural areas, and members of certain ethnic and religious groups as being at particular risk of being excluded from school. In addition to gender discrimination and poverty, early marriage was also indicated as a factor that negatively affected education levels.

In October, for the first time in six years, the government allowed UNICEF access to Golo, Jebel Marra in Central Darfur, to assess education needs. UNICEF reported 3,739 children in five schools and 9,000 out-of-school children needed urgent assistance, as the area had been inaccessible to humanitarian interventions since 2010.

Child Abuse: Child abuse and abduction for ransom were widespread in conflict areas and less prevalent in nonconflict areas. The government tried to enforce laws criminalizing child abuse and was more likely to prosecute cases involving child abuse and sexual exploitation of children than cases involving adults. Some police stations included family and child protection units that were "child friendly" and provided legal, medical, and psychosocial support for children. NGOs reported social stigma and lack of cooperation from some families prevented cases from being referred to police authorities.

Local NGOs reported an increase in street children and expressed concern that children working in public transportation and public markets were particularly vulnerable to sexual abuse and subsequent extortion. Due to shame and social stigma associated with sexual abuse, abused children often remained with their patrons out of fear of blackmail and were often too afraid to seek help. Early in the year, several newspapers were confiscated after they published a report highlighting the sexual abuse of minors on public buses.

Early and Forced Marriage: The law establishes the legal age of marriage at 10 years old for girls and 15 years old or puberty for boys. There were no reliable statistics on the extent of child marriage, but child advocates reported it remained a problem, especially in rural areas. According to UNICEF estimates, 12 percent of women between the ages 20 and 24 years old were first married or in a union before they were 15 years old, and 34 percent were married before reaching 18. The government adopted in December 2015 a draft national strategy to promote the abandonment of child marriage. The president's wife also launched an initiative in December to end child marriage. Throughout the year there continued to be consultative processes on the strategy between religious and political leaders.

Female Genital Mutilation and Cutting (FGM/C): Information on girls under 18 is provided in the women's section above.

Sexual Exploitation of Children: Penalties for offenses related to the sexual exploitation of children vary and can include imprisonment, fines, or both. Sexual exploitation of children was less prevalent in nonconflict areas. The government tried to enforce laws criminalizing sexual exploitation of children; NGOs reported, however, that social stigma prevented many families from pursuing legal cases against perpetrators. Some police stations included protection units that were "child friendly" and provided legal, medical, and psychosocial support for children.

There is no minimum age for consensual sex or statutory rape law. There were occurrences of nonconsensual sex with children who were forced into early marriage. Pornography, including child pornography, is illegal. Statutes prescribe a fine and period of imprisonment not to exceed 15 years for offenses involving child pornography.

Child prostitution also remained a problem, although the government denied the phenomenon existed in the country.

<u>Child Soldiers</u>: Armed groups continued to recruit and deploy child soldiers in internal conflicts (see section 1.g.).

<u>Displaced Children</u>: Internally displaced children often lacked access to government services such as health and education due to both security concerns and an inability to pay related fees. In October UNICEF reported approximately 70 percent of IDPs were children. In Darfur more than 200,000 persons were thought to have been internally displaced during the year, of whom at least 120,000 were estimated to be children. Of the 161 children recorded as unaccompanied IDPs, 11 were reunited with their families. According to UNHCR reports in November, more than 70 percent of the 263,245 total arrivals from South Sudan, who arrived after the outbreak of conflict in December 2013, were children (see section 2.d.). Children represented 60 percent of the 90,516 refugees who arrived from South Sudan since January.

<u>Institutionalized Children</u>: Police typically sent homeless children who had committed crimes to government camps for indefinite periods. Health care, schooling, and living conditions were generally very basic. All children in the camps, including non-Muslims, had to study the Quran. The government granted international and domestic humanitarian NGOs access to the camps. NGOs sometimes assisted the government with certain aspects of camp operations.

<u>International Child Abductions</u>: The country is not a party to the 1980 Hague Convention on the Civil Aspects of International Child Abduction. See the Department of State's *Annual Report on International Parental Child Abduction* at travel.state.gov/content/childabduction/en/legal/compliance.html.

Anti-Semitism

A very small Jewish community remained in the country, predominantly in the Khartoum area. While there were no reports of anti-Semitic acts, societal attitudes were not tolerant of Jewish persons.

Trafficking in Persons

See the Department of State's *Trafficking in Persons Report* at
www.state.gov/j/tip/rls/tiprpt/.

Persons with Disabilities

Although the law, including the Interim National Constitution, provides protection
for persons with disabilities, social stigma and a lack of resources hindered the
government's enforcement of disability laws. The law does not specifically
prohibit discrimination against persons with disabilities, but it stipulates, "The
State shall guarantee to persons with special needs the enjoyment of all the rights
and freedoms set out in the Constitution, access to suitable education [and]
employment, and participation in society."

In 2013 the Ministry of Social Welfare, Women, and Child Affairs and the
National Council for Persons with Disabilities launched an initiative to improve
access to public-sector jobs and encourage respect for the constitutional rights of
persons with disabilities. The Ministry of Education also established a special
education department. Children with disabilities attended public schools, and there
were some other educational institutions for persons with disabilities, including
two schools for persons with visual disabilities. In 2013 the Ministry of Education
initiated a national education strategy for 2013-16, which included specific
provisions for children with disabilities.

Social stigma and lack of resources often prevented government and private
entities from accommodating persons with disabilities in education and
employment. Appropriate supports were especially rare in rural areas.

The government has not enacted laws or implemented effective programs to
provide for access to buildings, information, and communication for persons with
disabilities. Persons with disabilities reported it was difficult to access or afford
necessary equipment, such as wheelchairs.

Several NGOs continued to advocate on behalf of persons with disabilities.

National/Racial/Ethnic Minorities

The population includes more than 500 ethnic groups, speaking numerous
languages and dialects. Many of these ethnic groups self-identify as Arab,
referring to their language and other cultural attributes. Other tribes self-identify,

or are identified by the broader society as African. Northern Muslims traditionally dominated the government. Interethnic fighting in Darfur was between Muslims who considered themselves either Arab or non-Arab and between different Arab tribes. "National Identity" is one of the six discussion committees of the national dialogue.

Some ethnic groups, such as the Beja in the eastern region, promoted a hierarchical social structure within their own ethnic groups that discriminated against persons of certain tribes. The Zaghawa ethnic group in Darfur maintained a caste system that discriminated against persons of lower castes.

The Muslim majority government continued to discriminate against ethnic and some religious minorities in almost every aspect of society. Citizens in Arabic-speaking areas who did not speak Arabic experienced discrimination in education, employment, and other areas (see section 7.d.).

The government announced that persons fleeing the conflicts in South Sudan should be considered "brothers and sisters" and thus not subjected to discrimination. Some South Sudanese returning to Sudan were able to reintegrate into their old Sudanese communities, but many reported it difficult to find employment. Most South Sudanese returnees settled in East Darfur and White Nile States. In conflict areas there were reports persons of South Sudanese origin experienced societal discrimination. Security forces often suspected persons of South Sudanese origin of supporting antigovernment forces in Abyei and the Two Areas.

Acts of Violence, Discrimination, and Other Abuses Based on Sexual Orientation and Gender Identity

Lesbian, gay, bisexual, transgender and intersex (LGBTI) persons are not considered a protected class under antidiscrimination laws. The law does not specifically prohibit homosexuality but criminalizes sodomy, which is punishable by death. Antigay sentiment was pervasive in society. LGBTI individuals expressed concern for their safety and did not identify themselves publicly. There was at least one confirmed case of an individual detained, beaten, and harassed by authorities because of his suspected affiliation with LGBTI-friendly groups. LGBTI organizations increasingly felt pressured to suspend or alter their activities due to threat of harm. Several LGBTI persons felt compelled to leave the country due to fear of persecution, intimidation, or harassment. Because unmarried women usually remained in the home of their parents until marriage, LGBTI women who were disowned by their families generally faced severe social stigma.

There were no reports of official action to investigate or punish those complicit in LGBTI-related discrimination or abuses.

HIV and AIDS Social Stigma

In August 2015 the Sudanese Society for HIV Victims disclosed there were 3,443 persons with HIV/AIDS in the country, including 1,693 men, 1,514 women, and 236 children. The organization reported it facilitated income-generating projects to support children of HIV-positive parents who could not afford school fees.

There was societal discrimination against persons with HIV/AIDS. The conservative nature of society made discussion of sex out of wedlock and related issues difficult, particularly for activists and members of the international community addressing these topics.

Promotion of Acts of Discrimination

The government, government-supported militias, and rebel groups reportedly promoted hatred and discrimination, using standard propaganda techniques. The government often used religiously charged language to refer to suspected antigovernment supporters.

The government did not take measures to counter hate speech.

Section 7. Worker Rights

a. Freedom of Association and the Right to Collective Bargaining

The law provides that employees of companies with more than 100 workers can form and join independent unions. Other employees can join nearby, preexisting unions. The law establishes a single national trade union federation and excludes police, military personnel, prison employees, legal advisers in the Justice Ministry, and judges from membership. In some cases membership in international unions was not officially recognized. The Sudan Workers' Trade Union Federation, a government-controlled federation of unions that consisted of 18 state unions and 22 industry unions, is the only official umbrella organization for unions. While there were no NGOs that specialized in broad advocacy for labor rights, there were "shadow unions" for most professions, although not recognized by the government. For example, the government recognized only the Sudan Journalists Union, whose membership included all journalists, including the spokesperson of the Sudan Air Force, as well as NISS media censorship officials. Most independent journalists, however, were members of the nonregistered Sudan Journalist Network, which organized advocacy activities on behalf of journalists.

The law denies trade unions autonomy to exercise the right to organize or to bargain collectively. It defines the objectives, terms of office, scope of activities, and organizational structures and alliances for labor unions. The government's auditor general supervised union funds because they are considered public money. The law provides unions the right to conduct legal strikes. Some unions have by-laws that self-restrict their right to strike. Labor observers believed some of these self-restrictions were imposed to maintain favor with the government. The law does not specifically prohibit strikes in nonessential sectors, but it requires all strikes to receive prior approval from the government after satisfying a set of legal requirements. Specialized labor courts adjudicate standard labor disputes, but the Ministry of Labor has the authority to refer a dispute to compulsory arbitration. Disputes also may be referred to arbitration if indicated in the work contract. The law does not prohibit antiunion discrimination by employers.

The government restricted the right to strike. Police could break up any strike conducted without prior government approval. In October and November, NISS detained 12 and summoned approximately 30 to 37 doctors participating in a strike to improve working conditions, protections, and training for doctors. As of December all but one doctor had been released. None was charged with any crime.

Bureaucratic steps mandated by law to resolve disputes within companies may be lengthy. Additionally court sessions may involve significant delays and costs when labor grievances are appealed.

The government did not effectively enforce applicable laws. Freedom of association and the right to collective bargaining were not respected (see section 1.e.). There were credible reports the government routinely intervened to manipulate professional, trade, and student union elections.

According to the International Trade Union Confederation, in oil-producing regions police and secret service agents, in collusion with oil companies, closely monitored workers' activities.

b. Prohibition of Forced or Compulsory Labor

The law prohibits all forms of forced or compulsory labor. The government, however, did not effectively enforce the law. Resources, inspections, and remediation were inadequate, and penalties for violations in the form of fines were rarely imposed and were insufficient to deter violations. Most of the violations existed in agricultural and pastoral sectors. Enforcement proved difficult in rural areas and areas undergoing conflict.

The government stated it investigated and prosecuted cases of forced labor, but it did not compile comprehensive statistics on the subject. Some government officials claimed that forced labor had been eradicated and denied reports that citizens engaged in this practice.

The forcible recruitment of persons into armed groups continued (see section 1.g.).

There were reports some children were engaged in forced labor, especially in the informal mining sector. Some domestic workers were believed to work under forced conditions or without pay. Women refugees were especially prone to labor violations. Also see the Department of State's *Trafficking in Persons Report* at www.state.gov/j/tip/rls/tiprpt/.

c. Prohibition of Child Labor and Minimum Age for Employment

The Interim National Constitution mandates that the state protect the rights of children as provided in international and regional conventions ratified by the country. The law defines children as persons younger than 18 years old but does not explicitly prohibit child labor. According to the Child Act, 12 years old is the minimum age children can be engaged in "light work." The Ministry of Social Welfare, Women, and Child Affairs is responsible for enforcing child labor laws.

The law prohibits the employment of young persons in hazardous industries and jobs, in jobs requiring significant physical effort, or in activities harmful to their morals. The law also prohibits the employment of young persons between 8 p.m. and 6 a.m., although authorities may exempt persons ages 15 and 16 years old from this restriction. It is illegal to employ children under age 12 years old, except in state vocational training schools and training workshops and jobs performed under apprenticeship contracts. Work supervised by family members that does not include nonfamily members, such as on family farms, is also excluded from these provisions.

The law allows minors to work for seven hours a day broken by a period of one paid hour of rest. It is illegal to compel minors to work more than four consecutive hours, work overtime, or work during weekly periods of rest or on official holidays. The law prohibits employers from waiving, postponing, or reducing annual leave entitlements. The government did not always enforce such laws due to inadequate resources to monitor work areas or overcome societal complicity.

Child labor was a serious problem, particularly in the agricultural and pastoral sectors where the practice was common. Most child labor occurred in the informal sector, including in menial jobs for which the government lacked the resources to monitor comprehensively. Children were engaged in shining shoes, washing and repairing cars, collecting medical and other resalable waste, street vending, begging, agricultural work, construction, and other menial labor. In January 2015 the National Council for Child Welfare reported that 22 percent of the country's children were engaged in child labor; as of August that number was still approximately 22 percent.

The International Labor Organization monitored the use of forced child labor in gold mining. UNICEF received unverified reports revealing the dangerous conditions children were working in gold mining, including the requirement to carry heavy loads, work at night and within confined spaces, and be exposed to mercury and high temperatures. There were reports children as young as 10 years old were used in artisanal gold mining throughout the country. According to multiple reputable sources, thousands of children worked in artisanal gold mining throughout the country, particularly in River Nile, Blue Nile, West Darfur, and North Darfur States, resulting in large numbers of students dropping out of school.

There were reports of the use of child soldiers by the SPLM-N, but numbers were difficult to verify. Also see section 1.g. and the Department of State's *Trafficking in Persons Report* at www.state.gov/j/tip/rls/tiprpt/.

d. Discrimination with Respect to Employment and Occupation

Law and regulations prohibit discrimination regarding race, sex, gender, disability, tribe, and language, but they do not protect classes according to sexual orientation or gender identity, HIV-positive status or other communicable diseases, political opinion, social or national origin, age, or social status. Labor laws apply to migrant workers with legal contracts, but foreign workers who are not considered to have legal status also are not provided legal protections from abuse and exploitation.

The government did not effectively enforce labor laws and regulations, and penalties in the form of fines were rarely imposed and were insufficient to deter violations. Discrimination in employment and occupation occurred based on gender, religion, and ethnic, tribal, or party affiliation. Ethnic minorities often complained that government hiring practices discriminated against them in favor of "riverine" Arabs from northern Sudan. Ethiopians, Eritreans, and other refugees or migrants were often exposed to exploitative work conditions. There were reports that some female refugees and migrants working as domestic workers or tea sellers were not compensated for their work, required to pay "kettle taxes" to police, sexually exploited, or trafficked. Due to their uncertain legal status, many refugees and migrants did not report cases of discrimination or abuse due to fear of imprisonment or repatriation.

Migrant workers and some ethnic minorities were unaware of their legal rights, suffered from discrimination, and lacked ready access to judicial remedies. The International Organization of Migration established a migrants' reception center in Khartoum that included workshops on workers' rights and the hazards of migration.

e. Acceptable Conditions of Work

The minimum monthly wage for public sector-workers was 425 SDG ($64). Normally the High Council of Salary in the Ministry of Cabinet Affairs sets the minimum wage for the public sector. The minimum monthly salary in the private sector is set by agreements made between individual industries and the High Council of Salary, and it varied among industries. Citizens whose monthly wages are below 700 SDG ($105) pay no personal income tax. An estimated 46 percent of citizens lived below the poverty line of 12 SDG ($1.80) per day.

The law limits the workweek to 40 hours (five eight-hour days, which does not include a 30-minute to one-hour daily break), with days of rest on Friday and Saturday. Overtime should not exceed 12 hours per week or four hours per day, although some persons worked longer than this limit on occasion. The law provides for paid annual leave after one year of continuous employment and paid holidays after three months.

The laws prescribe occupational safety and health standards. Any industrial company with between 30 and 150 employees must have an industrial safety officer. A larger company is required to have an industrial safety committee that includes management and employees. Committees and officers are required to report safety incidents to the Ministry of Labor. The law requires the owner of an industrial company to inform workers of occupational hazards and provide means for protection against such hazards. Management is also required to take necessary precautions to protect workers against industrial accidents and occupational diseases, but the law does not recognize the right of workers to remove themselves from dangerous work situations without loss of employment. Some heavy industry and artisanal mining operations, notably gold extraction, reportedly lacked sufficient safety regulations.

Safety laws do not apply to domestic servants; casual workers; agricultural workers other than those employed in the operation, repair, and maintenance of agricultural machinery; enterprises that process or market agricultural products such as cotton gins or dairy-product factories; jobs related to the administration of agricultural projects, including office work, accountancy, storage, gardening, and livestock husbandry; and family members of an employee who live with the employee and who are completely or partially dependent on him for their living.

Representatives of the Eritrean and Ethiopian communities in Khartoum stated undocumented migrants in the capital were subjected to abusive work conditions. They also reported many undocumented workers did not report abuse due to fear authorities might deport them to Eritrea because of their illegal status.

The Ministry of Labor, which maintained field offices in most major cities, is responsible for enforcing these standards. Various types of labor inspectors included specialists on labor relations, labor conflicts, and vocational, health, and recruitment practices. They operated on both federal and state levels.

Standards were not effectively enforced. Although employers generally respected the minimum wage law in the formal sector, in the informal sector wages could be significantly below the official rate. Since enforcement by the Ministry of Labor was minimal, working conditions generally were poor. Inspection efforts and enforcement were generally minimal in both the formal and informal sectors.

More than 10,000 women depended on selling tea on the streets of Khartoum State for their livelihoods after having fled conflict in Darfur and the Two Areas. Through her activism, Awadeya Mahmoud confronted government authorities, who often confiscated the women's belongings and fined them for working without permits. In response Mahmoud created the Women's Food and Tea Sellers' Cooperative of Khartoum State in 1990, which helped advocate for economic empowerment for women in Sudan's informal sector. In March, as a result of Mahmoud's advocacy, she received international recognition and was awarded by a foreign government and, in May, by the office of the vice president. The cooperative reported a significant decrease in harassments of tea ladies and confiscation of their belongings in the months following the awards, which shed light on the situation of tea ladies and raised awareness of harassment against them by authorities. By year's end, however, media reported that harassment incidents had increased to preaward levels.

Wage, overtime, and occupational safety and health standards violations were common in the industrial and informal labor sectors, especially in the areas of agriculture and pastoral work. Foreign migrant workers, youth, and female workers typically faced the most exploitative working conditions. An estimated 60 percent of the workforce worked in the informal sector, according to the *2012 Africa Economic Outlook*. There was no credible data on workplace fatalities and accidents.